AID THAT COUNTS

Solon Barraclough, Ariane van Buren, Alicia Gariazzo,
Anjali Sundaram, Peter Utting

AID THAT COUNTS

THE WESTERN CONTRIBUTION TO DEVELOPMENT AND SURVIVAL IN NICARAGUA

Transnational Institute (TNI)
Coordinadora Regional de Investigaciones Económicas y Sociales
(CRIES)

First published in 1988 by Transnational Institute,
Paulus Potterstraat 20, 1071 DA Amsterdam, The Netherlands,
and
Third World Publications, 151 Stratford Road, Birmingham B11 1RD,
United Kingdom

Cover, text design, and map by Marijke Mooy, Amsterdam, The Netherlands
Typeset by Grassroots, London, U.K.
Cover printed by Rob Stolk, Amsterdam, The Netherlands
Printed by EPO, Antwerp, Belgium

British Library Cataloguing in Publication Data

Aid that Counts : the Western Contribution
to development and survival in Nicaragua.
1. Nicaragua. Economic development. Foreign assistance
I. Barraclough, Solon II. Transnational Institute.
388.91'097285

ISBN 0-907108-94-6

Distributed in the U.S. by the Institute for Policy Studies,
1901 Que Street, N.W., Washington D.C. 20009, USA

NICARAGUA

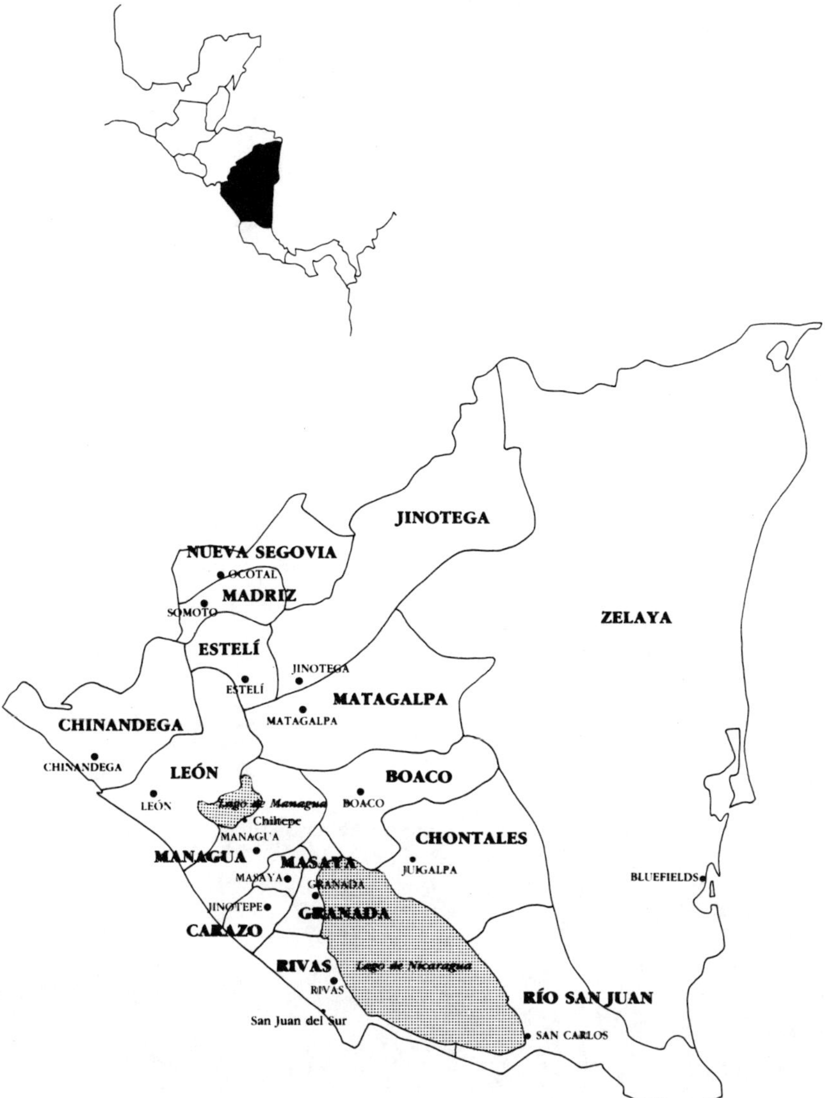
JINOTEGA
NUEVA SEGOVIA
OCOTAL
MADRIZ
SOMOTO
ZELAYA
ESTELÍ
JINOTEGA
ESTELÍ
MATAGALPA
MATAGALPA
CHINANDEGA
CHINANDEGA
LEÓN
BOACO
LEÓN
Lago de Managua
Chiltepe
BOACO
MANAGUA
CHONTALES
MANAGUA
MASAYA
JUIGALPA
MASAYA
GRANADA
BLUEFIELDS
JINOTEPE
GRANADA
CARAZO
RIVAS
Lago de Nicaragua
RIVAS
RÍO SAN JUAN
San Juan del Sur
SAN CARLOS

Contents

LIST OF TABLES

List of Tables

Acknowledgements

We want to thank all the people we interviewed for this study, for their cooperation and assistance. Special thanks must go to Carlos Arce who, when the study began, was Director of Planning of the Nicaraguan Ministry of External Cooperation. He not only gave us access to data but also provided a frank assessment of trends and problems associated with foreign aid. Many people helped us organize field trips to visit project sites, but we are particularly grateful to Maryann Jackman, late Director of the Office of International Relations and External Cooperation for the Department of Matagalpa, who died in a tragic road accident shortly after helping us with this research.

Much support was provided by our colleagues, and associates of the Transnational Institute. Xabier Gorostiaga and the staff of CRIES assisted with arrangements and information in Managua. Marie Duflo, John Mensley of the OECD, Elfriede Uhr, and others helped procure information in Europe. John Cavanagh, Lord Pratap Chitnis, E.V.K. Fitzgerald, Susan George, George Irvin, and Basker Vashee provided valuable comments on the text. Edgard Pisani and Jan Pronk reviewed the text prior to publication. Jacquelynn Craw and Sara Henley expedited the editing and production of this book. Our thanks go warmly to each and all.

The study was financed through generous grants from the Norwegian Ministry for Development Cooperation, the Netherlands Organization for International Development (NOVIB), the Humanistic Institute for Cooperation with Developing Countries (HIVOS), SWISSAID, Trocaire, the Swedish International Development Authority (SIDA), Christian Aid, the World Council of Churches, Oxfam 'UK', Danish Church Aid, and the Funding Exchange in the United States. We hope that this study, which provides tangible evidence of what can be achieved with such collaboration, will encourage these donors to strengthen their own programmes and to give each other mutual support.

Amsterdam
October 1987

PREFACE

The terrible turmoil in Central America in recent years has obscured what Nicaragua represented to the international development community only a short while ago. Through nationwide campaigns, Nicaraguan citizens were engaged in developing their own literacy, health care, and in creating a better future. Economic development plans stressed an internal reorientation towards the needs of Nicaraguans as a whole, and externally, an expanding of relations with new parts of the world.

European governments and non-governmental organizations actively assisted this process because, despite inevitable flaws, it embraced many of the democratic and participatory principles that we view as integral to development.

Now, the five presidents of Central America have concurred in the first real possibility of peace in years. It is of utmost importance that we do all we can to speed that process along with our political support, and create a climate conducive to peace. In the next few years, the mammoth task of rebuilding the economies of the region will be the priority—and crucial if a strong basis for democracy is to be created.

This is especially the case in Nicaragua, where the economy has been badly undermined in the attempt to survive in the face of war. External assistance has played a vital role in that survival, just as it has done in enabling investment for future development. We must now come forth with the further assistance needed to get the economy moving again and the hundreds of thousands of displaced people resettled.

This report sketches the evolution of the Nicaraguan development strategy, and analyses how European and other external assistance has supported that development. It also lays out the difficulties and needs of the present 'survival economy', and assesses the extent to which international assistance has adapted to changing priorities.

The report offers a major challenge to European governments, development agencies and non-governmental organizations: to appreciate the difficulties in Nicaragua and bolster assistance to it, particularly at this delicate moment when there seems at last to be a way out of the great suffering which has been inflicted.

Let us take up that challenge.

Lord Chitnis
House of Lords, Great Britain
16th October, 1987

INTRODUCTION

This is an examination of external assistance to Nicaragua since the 1979 revolution. It presents the findings of a study which the Transnational Institute (TNI) undertook in 1986, in collaboration with the Central American Regional Coordinating Body for Economic and Social Research (CRIES). In particular, it scrutinizes the contributions that Western Europe and Canada have made, compared with those of other parts of the world. It analyses how the nature of these contributions has changed as Nicaragua's priorities have shifted, from an initial emphasis on reconstruction after the revolution, to long-term development investment, and now a 'survival economy' in the face of mounting economic and military pressure.

World attention focused on the tiny country of Nicaragua in 1979, when popular insurrections in its major cities marked the culmination of a prolonged guerilla struggle to overthrow the 45-year-old dictatorship of the Somoza family and its National Guard. When the Sandinistas finally defeated the Somoza forces and installed a broad-based National Junta of Reconstruction to govern the country on 19th July 1979, the economy was in ruins.

Extensive fighting had badly damaged Nicaragua's infrastructure. Its earnings from agro-exports—the principal source of foreign exchange—had been considerably reduced by the war, and by falling commodity prices on world markets. Between 1977 and 1979, gross domestic product (GDP) fell by almost one-third. To reconstruct the country, and begin a process of economic development whereby the basic needs of the long-neglected majority of the population could be met, incalculable quantities of external resources and technical assistance were needed.

The international community responded generously with emergency aid. In the second half of 1979 alone, $83 million[1] were given in official (bilateral and multilateral) grants and $272 million in loans. Over the next seven years, international assistance averaged some $600 million annually—far more than Nicaragua's yearly exports. This was substantial for a country of only three million people.

Considerable assistance came from Western Europe and Canada, amounting to about a fifth of the total. In late 1986, however, there were indications that several Western European governments might sharply reduce aid: due to their own domestic budgetary constraints, changing internal political alignments, and pressures from the Reagan administration to cut off aid in order to help undermine Nicaragua's economy and facilitate the overthrow of its government by counter-revolutionary or Contra forces. These disquieting signals, and the absence of any comprehensive review of international cooperation with Nicaragua, prompted the present study.

Objectives

One objective of the study is to help Western European governments and non-governmental organizations (NGOs) providing assistance to Nicaragua to see their contributions in relation to overall international cooperation with Nicaragua. The study records the range of sources and the different uses of foreign aid. A second objective is to assess the compatibility of European aid programmes with Nicaraguan national priorities and development objectives, which have evolved in response to economic constraints and the war. A third is to examine the operation and impact of a few typical projects receiving Western European and Canadian support. Fourth, the study aims to bring the debate on development assistance and its role in Nicaragua to a wider, non-specialized audience.

The report is intended primarily for Western governments, parliamentarians, aid agencies, NGOs, and the interested public. It provides a thorough overview of development assistance in Nicaragua, and an independent assessment of the effectiveness of development efforts, mapping out the obstacles encountered. It is not an exhaustive evaluation of projects. Instead it is offered as an indicator of the role Western aid can play in promoting autonomous development in the Third World.

Structure of the Book

The book has a 'telescopic' structure. Parts I, II, and III are each intended for different audiences wanting different levels of detail.

Part I is a short *summary* of the study's principal conclusions for readers with time for only a few pages.

Part II is a longer *overview*, highlighting major trends in international cooperation with Nicaragua. It is meant for people looking for the central findings of the study.

Part III gives a *detailed analysis* in four chapters. Chapter 1 reviews the phases of Nicaraguan reconstruction and development policies from 1979 to 1986. It shows how policies changed in response to experience, to world economic recession, to the U.S. economic blockade and support of Contra aggression, and to internal social forces.

Chapter 2 looks at the total contribution of international assistance. It focuses on the structure and sources of cooperation, from multilateral agencies, OECD countries, developing countries, and the socialist bloc.

Chapter 3 examines the role of Western European and Canadian aid in greater detail. It discusses the trends in quantity and forms of aid, including that from NGOs.

Chapter 4 assesses the implementation of five projects assisted by Western Europe and Canada.

Five appendices give supplementary information about the people we interviewed, the projects financed by Western Europe and Canada, and the terms of official loans and credits, as well as data on donations by NGOs and other sources.

Methods and Definitions

In September 1986, interviews were conducted in Nicaragua with representatives of international donor agencies in Nicaragua, their Nicaraguan counterparts, and government officials responsible for planning or administrating aid. Development assistance data, evaluations, and project descriptions were collected, and project sites visited. In Europe, information about cooperation with Nicaragua was obtained from governments, NGOs and intergovernmental bodies. A detailed technical report was drafted in early 1987, reviewed in Europe and Nicaragua, and discussed with representatives of the donor agencies.

One of the problems encountered in this research concerned the definition of 'aid'. Aid was defined broadly to include monetary and non-monetary grants and donations, as well as concessionary credits, loans and technical assistance. This definition roughly corresponds with the term 'external cooperation' used by the Nicaraguan government. While much of the literature on aid focuses primarily on grants, the dividing line between concessionary loans and donations is unclear. For example, Canadian bilateral assistance to Nicaragua consists of loans with terms of repayment which are so 'soft', or concessionary, that although they are formally classified as loans, in fact they amount to a 95 percent donation.

Some analysts equate 'aid' with *official* development assistance.[2]

The concept of external cooperation, however, is broader. It includes grants from private voluntary organizations and solidarity groups. As these are numerous in Nicaragua, it is important to incorporate them in an analysis of aid.

The study makes no attempt to estimate or discuss military aid, which is outside its brief. Data on sources, volumes, and uses of military assistance are in any case either inadequate or unavailable.

Even on development assistance, data are often inconsistent or unavailable. Information on commitments of official multilateral and bilateral aid does exist in the Nicaraguan Ministry of External Cooperation and other sources such as the EEC, although such data are not always fully compatible with each other. Data on actual *disbursements* of aid, however, are not readily available from the Nicaraguan government. Nevertheless, some information on disbursements was obtained from the OECD.

It is even more difficult to estimate the nature and importance of aid through countless NGOs, solidarity groups and the like. In the early years after the revolution there was much of this sort of aid—but it was never recorded centrally, and sometimes not at all. Since early 1986 the Nicaraguan government has begun registering all aid of this kind, but as yet, its records are incomplete. In just one of the country's 16 departments, for example, over 500 such projects are known to exist, but for most there are no records of size, purpose, donor and recipient organizations, local and foreign funds, and numbers of local and foreign personnel. The report's estimate of the quantity of external aid involved must therefore be seen as tentative and approximate.

Another difficulty arose in the selection and assessment of a few 'typical' development projects benefiting from Western European or Canadian aid. The report includes brief accounts of five projects. They represent five different sectors—agriculture, distribution of basic products, education, health, and communications—and range widely in size, location, and the type of donor. They are illustrative cases, and not meant as a representative sample. The researchers used whatever evaluative materials could be obtained, either from donor organizations or elsewhere, and supplemented these with interviews with project personnel. The report gives descriptions of the projects, together with judgements and hypotheses about their impact. It does not pretend to present fully detailed evaluations.

Assessing the effectiveness of aid presents further conceptual problems. The criteria one would use depend on the normative view one takes of 'development'. In this study, development implies much more than merely raising the rate of economic growth and level of average income per capita. It means people having sufficient livelihood to lead an adequate life. Those groups that have been poor and powerless should furthermore be able to participate in decisions which influence their lives. Development requires a guarantee of human rights, democratic participation, and a measure of political, cultural, and economic autonomy. Development should improve the use of a country's human and natural resources independent of foreign control. These values generally coincide with those of the international consensus expressed in numerous UN resolutions, and with those of post-revolutionary development policy in Nicaragua.

About the Authors

The study was conducted by independent researchers with extensive experience in development assistance. In Nicaragua, Peter Utting coordinated the research and, with Alicia Gariazzo, prepared the technical report. He is an Australian social scientist, has been based in Nicaragua since 1979, and works as a principal researcher at the Centre for Research and Studies on Agrarian Reform (CIERA). He has carried out extensive research on economic policy in Nicaragua in cooperation with international agencies, and is a consultant to the United Nations Research Institute for Social Development (UNRISD). Alicia Gariazzo is a Chilean economist, who has worked in Nicaragua since 1981 with the Nicaraguan Economic and Social Research Institute (INIES) and other Nicaraguan agencies. Utting and Gariazzo are Associate Fellows of the Transnational Institute (TNI). Anjali Sundaram, Fellow of the TNI and Coordinator of its Central America Project since 1985, carried out research in Europe, reported on site visits to development projects in Nicaragua, and helped prepare the final report.

The study was directed by Solon Barraclough, former Director of the United Nations Research Institute for Social Development (UNRISD) and head of aid missions to Nicaragua for UNRISD, the International Fund for Agricultural Development (IFAD), and Oxfam America. He is also an Associate Fellow of the Transnational Institute. The project was supervised and the final report edited by Ariane van Buren, Director of the TNI and its Central America Project. A former consultant to IFAD, the Commonwealth Fund for Technical Cooperation in Tanzania, Senegal, and China, her work in Nicaragua includes direction of research on the management of energy resources for the Swedish International Development

Authority (SIDA) and the Nicaraguan Institute of Natural Resources and Environment.

NOTES

1. All figures in dollars refer to U.S. dollars.
2. See, for example, R. Cassen and Associates, *Does Aid Work?*, Oxford University Press, Oxford, U.K., 1986, p.2.

PART I:

MAIN CONCLUSIONS

Main conclusions

○ External economic cooperation with post-revolutionary Nicaragua has been substantial: from mid-1979 to 1986, it totalled $4,618 million in medium- and long-term loans and credits, and in bilateral, multilateral and non-governmental grants, averaging about $600 million a year.

○ These external resources have played a vital role in enabling the Nicaraguan government to undertake substantial programmes of social improvement and longer-term productive investment. They have also been crucial in restoring the losses in production and infrastructure resulting from the 1978-79 war, and from more recent Contra attacks and U.S. economic pressures. However, this aid has also sown the seeds of future problems. First, the consequent external debt exceeded $5 billion in 1986—which is nearly twice the total Gross National Product (GNP), and about $1,500 per capita. Servicing the debt is a considerable financial burden. Second, food imports are now more than double their pre-1979 level: Nicaragua must rapidly stimulate peasant production of basic foods, if the security of future food supply is not to be endangered. Third, though large public-sector investments made in capital-intensive agro-industrial and energy projects can contribute to greater autonomy in the future, they absorb scarce resources which might be better employed in stimulating production in other sectors, and they drain foreign exchange for imports of spare parts, replacements, and inputs to keep these projects opperating.

The impact of this debt, and of Nicaragua's dependence on intermediate and capital-goods imports, will be a function of world market conditions, of the country's ability to develop and diversify its economy, and of the terms on which aid is granted. The international community—and Europe and Canada in particular—can play a crucial role in refinancing the existing debt, and in preventing the blockage of loans from multilateral institutions.

○ About one-fifth of external aid has come from Western Europe and Canada. Another fifth consists of credits for petroleum imports, which were supplied by Mexico and Venezuela until 1982; by Mexico alone through 1984; and from the socialist bloc thereafter. The remaining 60 percent of the aid has come from multilateral sources (whose contribution has decreased sharply since 1980, under pressure from the United States), from Third World countries, and increasingly from the socialist bloc. Just as Nicaragua has obtained aid from a wide variety of sources, it has also diversified its trading partners. Western Europe, the socialist bloc countries, and some Latin American countries have replaced the United States and Central America as Nicaragua's principal trading partners.

○ Total Western European and Canadian loans, credits, and grants have averaged around $120 million annually in new commitments over 1980-86. Of this, about $60 million has been in the form of loans and credits. Governmental and EEC grants have amounted to another $31 million per year, excluding certain donations in kind. Substantial grants have also been made through non-governmental organizations (NGOs), solidarity groups and twin-city programmes, amounting to $30-50 million a year, mostly from Western Europe and Canada, but these include some official aid channelled through NGOs.

○ Western European and Canadian commitments of aid to Nicaragua have been erratic from year to year. Actual disbursements have flowed at a more stable rate, however, at least until 1986. The fluctuations in new commitments appear to be related to U.S. pressure, to changing internal political alignments and budget constraints in donor countries, and to variations in the quality and quantity of projects submitted by the Nicaraguan government. There has also been some inconsistency among certain governments, which have supported Nicaragua through bilateral programmes, yet their representatives to multilateral agencies have voted against loans to the same country. The unpredictability of aid levels presents difficulties to Nicaraguan planners who are attempting to improve the use of external resources.

○ New loans and credits from Western Europe and Canada fell sharply in 1986—although grants and actual disbursements of previous commitments increased. There is a danger now that Western aid could diminish, despite a steady improvement in Nicaragua's use of this aid, and Nicaragua's critical economic circumstances. Western donors should note that their aid is crucial in helping Nicaragua maintain pluralistic external alignments. Nicaragua has also succeeded in attracting assistance from sources other than conventional donors, notably Spain, Greece, China, and India.

○ Unlike multilateral and bilateral aid, aid from NGOs in Western Europe and North America shows no sign of decreasing—indeed it seems even to have grown in recent years. NGOs have supported projects of all sizes, but they have played a particularly important role in supporting relatively small participatory local projects. This kind of aid to popular organizations is important in building up a democratic civil society.

○ Despite its considerable political, economic, and social importance, NGO aid has attracted certain criticisms. For some years, a lack of coordination between NGO donors impeded effective administration of their aid. Until recently the government has not had the capacity to monitor all such aid or ensure its compatibility with national priorities. Better government accounting procedures would help assure donors that their contributions reach the appropriate destinations. While relations between NGOs and *local* authorities have been generally excellent, the *central* government has often underrated NGO aid, showing a preference for larger capital-intensive projects, and a concern over the presence of a large number of foreigners. There are now signs, however, that criticisms of NGO aid are being addressed by both donors and recipients.

○ 'Town-twinning' between Europe and Nicaragua has been important, not only politically but probably also economically. It has provided an avenue for local European assistance, and a channel for those donors who have no infrastructure in Nicaragua for disbursement. Where numerous towns in Europe have been twinned with the same town in Nicaragua, they have often joined forces and coordinated their actions internationally.

○ When compared with aid to most developing countries, Western aid to Nicaragua since the revolution has been well used in meeting development objectives. There has been a high degree of compatibility between the development goals of the government and those of many bilateral aid agencies, some multilateral agencies such as the EEC, those within the UN system, and most NGOs. The improvement in Nicaragua's aid record since the revolution has been facilitated by the government's commitment to basic needs and by the presence in Nicaragua of active popular organizations. This study's assessment of five typical development projects supported by Western Europe and Canada highlights many of the problems encountered, but concludes that their implementation has been relatively successful in meeting their objectives. Dialogue between the government and donors since 1979 has had a significant impact on the formulation and execution of some Nicaraguan development policies.

○ There is still room for considerable improvement in the administration and use of external resources in Nicaragua and much inefficiency has emerged. In recent years, however, and despite wartime conditions, progress has been made in administering aid, in planning its allocation in accordance with national priorities, and in overseeing its disbursement and use.

○ Western European and Canadian aid has gradually adapted quite well (though not always as quickly as one would hope) to the Nicaraguan government's change in priorities—from reconstruction and social improvement in 1979-81, to productive longer-term investments in 1982-84, and to defence and survival from 1985 onwards. Now, given a real possibility of peace, it is vital that governments and NGOs continue to adapt aid in line with changing priorities. The major task is to rebuild the local, regional and national economies. Given the changing context of aid, it would be timely and useful now to bring all Nicaragua's donors together in consultation. This has never been done, despite the large number of donors and the amount of aid they have given. Such a consultation could stimulate better coordination of aid, both by the Nicaraguan government and by donors. Moreover, a donors' review of the vast experience acquired in Nicaragua would help in designing their national and regional aid programmes throughout Central America, and elsewhere.

PART II:

MAJOR TRENDS IN INTERNATIONAL ASSISTANCE TO NICARAGUA

MAJOR TRENDS IN INTERNATIONAL ASSISTANCE TO NICARAGUA

A more detailed analysis of major trends can be found in Part III.

Aid from Western Europe and Canada, in the form of concessionary loans and credits, grants, and technical assistance, was vital to Nicaragua's reconstruction after the 1979 revolution. Since 1981, in the face of mounting aggression by the U.S.-backed Contras and growing economic pressure from the United States, which culminated in a trade embargo in 1985, this external assistance has furthermore played a crucial role in enabling the Nicaraguan government to survive—and to make longer-term investments for future development. Between 1979 and 1986, Western European and Canadian aid accounted for about one-fifth of all grants and medium and long-term loans and credits extended to Nicaragua.

The Nicaraguan government has been flexible in adapting to changing economic and political conditions, and serious problems have been faced with realism and imaginativeness. In a lengthy interview with the Sandinista newspaper *Barricada*, the Minister of External Cooperation recently called for major improvements in the government's organization, efficiency and accountability in using foreign aid.[1] He emphasised that foreign credits and grants constitute a precious and scarce resource, which should be used more efficiently to supplement national efforts in development and survival.

Many donors have also adapted their aid to the changing priorities in Nicaragua: from rebuilding after the revolution and meeting basic needs, to longer-term productive investment, and—since 1985—to maintaining a survival economy. Donors have increasingly recognized that conditions of war and economic crisis require a change in standard formulas of the kind of aid given and how it is disbursed—especially the conventional emphasis on large-scale investment projects. Some donor countries have also used the U.S. trade embargo as an opportunity to increase their own trade with Nicaragua.

The Role of International Cooperation

External cooperation with Nicaragua since 1979 has shown six principal trends. In the first place, the level of external assistance has increased. Second, sources of external cooperation changed markedly between 1979 and 1987. Third, Nicaragua's foreign trading partners have changed in accordance with the new patterns of external cooperation—but with some time-lag. Fourth, the types and uses of external resources have evolved, adjusting to the country's changing development policies and to world conditions. Fifth, the administration of aid has become better organized and more efficient. Sixth, external aid has been used relatively effectively to meet the post-revolutionary government's objectives of meeting basic needs, increasing popular participation, and building a more autonomous and diversified economy. Each of these trends is expanded below.

Levels of External Cooperation

The total of external financing can be deduced from the size of Nicaragua's trade and balance-of-payments deficits. The trade deficit, which averaged a little over $100 million annually from 1974 to 1977, has exceeded $370 million in every year since 1980, reaching $594 million in 1985 and $657 million in 1986 (see Table 3). Practically no private foreign investments or non-trade earnings entered Nicaragua over those years—other than limited remittances from citizens working abroad. The balance-of-payments deficit was therefore financed almost entirely by external financial assistance of one form or another—loans, credits, debt re-negotiation and grants. Such funds came to Nicaragua as aid, or to promote foreign trade—not in response to attractive interest rates or investment opportunities.

Other figures show that from mid-1979 to the end of 1986, the sum of all grants and new medium and long-term loans and credits reached $4,618 million, averaging about $600 million annually. Of this, loans and credits came to about $495 million a year in new commitments, although actual disbursements were probably somewhat lower. Officially recorded grants amounted to another $90 million per year, excluding some grants in kind and most NGO grants. The total is consistent with the balance-of-payments deficits over the period. The total of the new loans and credits corresponds to the increase in external debt (less capitalized interest charges), which expanded from $1.6 billion in mid-1979 to $5.3 billion at the end of 1986.

SOURCES OF EXTERNAL COOPERATION

Immediately following the revolution, international aid arrived from a wide variety of sources: regional and international agencies such as the Inter-American Development Bank and World Bank, other Latin American countries, the United States, and Western Europe. Only about 5 percent of the loans, credits, and grants received during 1979 and 1980 came from COMECON countries; while 43 percent came from multilateral agencies, 11 percent from Western Europe, 10 percent from the United States, and 22 percent from other Latin American countries.

This pattern changed rapidly after 1980. U.S. aid, including credits for wheat imports, ceased in that year. New loans from some international and regional agencies decreased sharply, falling to less than half their 1980 levels during 1981, 1982 and 1983—and, under U.S. pressure, ceased entirely in 1984. However, some multilateral support was maintained, totalling $20 million annually. This was composed of grants from the EEC and U.N. agencies such as UNICEF, UNDP, WFP and WHO, which found the government's social objectives and norms in the use of aid compatible with their own.

The Third World emerged in this period as a major new source of aid. According to Nicaraguan government figures, Panama provided more aid in the form of grants in 1979 than any West or East European government apart from Spain. In 1980, grants from Mexico far exceeded those of any other bilateral or multilateral source. Loans and credits from Latin American countries peaked in 1981 at $332 million (44 percent of the total that year). Most of these were credits for petroleum imports from Venezuela and Mexico. However, Venezuela ended its concessionary credits for petroleum imports in 1982 and Mexico followed in 1984, apparently under pressure from the U.S. and the IMF. New credits from Latin American sources amounted to only $25 million in 1985 and 1986. About 4 percent of all loans and credits since 1979 came from Asian and African countries: principally Libya, Iran, China, and India.

From 1980 onwards, the COMECON countries, Yugoslavia, and China began to replace the grants, loans and credits withdrawn by other sources. They supplied nearly one-third of the total in 1981-1983, and, on average approximately two-thirds in 1984-1986. Over the entire period from 1979 to 1986, the countries of the socialist bloc provided an average of 42 percent of all loans and credits, and 28 percent of all grants including those from NGOs. In 1985 new loans from these countries together with those from Western Europe trebled, in response to a reduction in multilateral lending, the suspension of Mexican petroleum credits, and the U.S. trade embargo.

Nicaragua obtained a major part of these loans and credits on highly concessionary terms. This is reflected by the fact that in 1986, although Nicaragua had the highest external debt in Latin America, per capita or as a percentage of GNP or export revenues, its interest payments were relatively low. The socialist bloc countries often charged higher interest rates on loans and credits than did than did Western Europe and Canada—but were generally more flexible in rescheduling repayments. Socialist bloc countries also frequently offered Nicaragua preferential prices for its exports, and lower-priced imports than the OECD countries (although exact comparisons are difficult because the currencies are non-convertible and the quality of products different).

Assistance from NGOs became increasingly important after the revolution. Voluntary agencies of all sorts encountered highly receptive local counterparts, and a close correspondence between their own social objectives and those of the government and the aid recipients. Their assistance has probably amounted to an average of $30-50 million annually. However, since some of the NGOs' funds come from official bilateral and multilateral sources, not all of the $30-50 million can be considered additional to the total of official aid.

CHANGING PATTERNS OF TRADE AND DEPENDENCY

The diversification of sources of external cooperation after 1979 was accompanied by parallel changes in the direction of foreign trade. Before the revolution, in 1974-77, trade with the United States accounted for one-fourth of Nicaragua's exports and 29 percent of imports. Trade with the other Western industrialized (OECD) economies represented 39 percent of exports and 27 percent of imports. The Central American Common Market provided most of the rest (about one-fifth of the total), while other developing countries accounted for 12 percent of exports and 22 percent of imports, which came mostly from Mexico and South America. Before 1980, there was virtually no trade with the socialist bloc.

Trade with the United States declined after 1980 and practically disappeared following the 1985 embargo. Trade with the Central American Common Market also fell, to only about 5 percent of the total by 1986. Imports from the rest of Latin America (excluding Cuba) more than doubled by 1983, but then dropped sharply following the termination of credits for petroleum imports from Mexico in 1984 and the financial crisis affecting nearly all countries in the region. Western Europe, Canada and other OECD countries (excluding the United States) purchased three-fourths of Nicaragua's exports and supplied a quarter of its imports during 1985-86. Socialist bloc countries provided nearly half Nicaragua's imports and purchased one-fifth of its exports in 1986.

Western and Eastern European countries have now replaced the United States and the other Central American countries as Nicaragua's principal trading partners. At the same time, economic difficulties related in part to the war and the U.S. embargo caused a fall in the value of Nicaraguan exports—to about half of their 1980 value in current terms by 1986. The value of imports has remained almost constant, making the country increasingly dependent on external financial cooperation.

These changes in Nicaragua's trade patterns and a growing dependency on external assistance carry both positive and negative implications for the country's future development. On the positive side, Nicaragua's former dependence on U.S. markets and financing has been broken, thereby reducing the country's vulnerability to U.S. political and economic pressure. Moreover, the terms of new loans and credits have been favourable to Nicaragua, as have been those under which the external debt was re-negotiated. The prices paid by socialist bloc countries for Nicaraguan exports have frequently been well above world market levels, although payment may not be in hard currency.

The disadvantages of the changes in Nicaragua's external economic relations include the greater transport costs incurred in trading with Europe, compared with the Americas—especially with neighbouring Central American countries. It is also costly for a small country to use different kinds of imported equipment which are not fully compatible with each other.

Nicaragua's dependence on external assistance has created other problems since most major aid donors, whether capitalist or socialist, prefer to finance large capital-intensive high-technology projects, rather than more mundane investments and current needs. This tendency has limited the Nicaraguan government's flexibility in year-to-year economic planning, since important segments of external and domestic resources have been tied up in projects that will not be completed, or yield returns, for many years. These investments also imply future costs for imported inputs and replacement parts as well as debt-servicing. Finally, Nicaragua is still highly vulnerable to economic and political events completely beyond its control, such as the reduction of aid by some Western European countries, and of petroleum exports by certain COMECON countries.

COMPOSITION AND USE OF EXTERNAL RESOURCES

Whereas many sources furnished aid after the revolution, no integrated national economic plan was prepared until 1980, and it was not until much later that effective mechanisms were developed to evaluate the proposed uses of external resources, and direct them towards national priorities. Various Nicaraguan ministries, agencies and organizations proposed projects to multilateral, bilateral, and NGO donors, resulting in a wide assortment of uncoordinated initiatives, characterized by the common interest of particular donors and recipients. Both Nicaraguan agencies and foreign donors gave priority to immediate reconstruction, popular needs, and longer-term productive and social investments; but rationalizing the use of available resources was necessarily slow and initially somewhat chaotic.

During 1979-81 many grants were provided in kind, such as food, trucks, machinery, and medicines. By 1980, food imports were double their 1978 level and thereafter higher than in pre-revolutionary years. Petroleum remained the biggest single import—amounting to a cost of about $145 million annually from 1981 to 1983. Several internationally assisted projects which had been started before the revolution were continued, such as the revival of diseased coffee plantations and the construction of new markets in Managua. Machinery, transport and equipment were replaced. Considerable external resources went into social programmes, such as health clinics, schools, and the literacy programme. Some longer-term investments to increase future production and exports were made in agriculture and agro-industry. A major project to develop geothermal energy resources was undertaken with important Italian assistance.

In accordance with the government's changing priorities, after 1981 a much higher proportion of external resources went into longer-term investments. Imports of capital goods for agriculture and agro-industry reached over $50 million per year—five times the pre-revolutionary level. Irrigation projects, oil palm plantations, sugar refining, fruit and vegetable processing, and high-technology dairy production received substantial external resources.

In 1985 the government was forced by the war to adopt a survival strategy. A higher proportion of external resources had to be used to import basic consumer goods, spare parts, replacements for worn-out equipment, and basic inputs for industry and agriculture. Some donors found it difficult to adjust to this change in priorities. Their aid bureaucracies often had rather rigid norms, requiring them to give priority to investments that would contribute directly to greater future national product, or to specific social objectives.

Many donors understood the situation, however, and modified their aid to meet the government's changing priorities. France and Spain increased commercial credits to Nicaragua for the import of vital repair parts, machinery replacements, crucial production inputs and some essential consumer goods previously imported from the United States but also manufactured by transnational enterprises in Western Europe. Sweden and other Nordic countries greatly increased aid, with few conditions attached. The socialist bloc countries increased assistance considerably, and adapted it to changing needs in Nicaragua.

ADMINISTRATION OF EXTERNAL RESOURCES

In 1979, the government established the International Reconstruction Fund (FIR) to seek, receive, and allocate official development assistance. The following year, The Augusto César Sandino Foundation (FACS), was established to seek aid from non-governmental, humanitarian and solidarity organizations, help Nicaraguan mass organizations prepare fundable projects, and oversee the use of this aid.

FIR played a valuable role in securing external resources, but did not have the necessary political authority or technical capacity to exercise much influence over their allocation, or supervise their use. FIR was strengthened in 1982, however, when the Department of Technical Cooperation of the Planning Ministry (MIPLAN) was transferred to its control. In that year, MIPLAN's Department of Socialist Countries began drawing up long-term guidelines for future cooperation with COMECON countries. The investment department of MIPLAN and an inter-ministerial commission began to evaluate project proposals in order to steer external resources towards national priorities. While these administrative changes helped, FIR still lacked sufficient clout to influence the interplay of large Nicaraguan ministries and foreign donors, and assure that the use of resources was fully compatible with the national economic plan. In 1985 the three MIPLAN departments were fused with FIR to form the Ministry of External Cooperation, which now has more authority and the technical resources to bring the use of external assistance into line with national priorities.

Coordinating and setting priorities for NGO aid, has been slower and more difficult, however. The NGOs initially dealt directly with local governments to avoid bureaucratic delays in FACS, but gradually FACS' capacity to deal with NGOs and help determine their priorities has grown. Nevertheless, in 1986 FACS had only 30 staff members handling all project design and fund-raising, as well as overseeing the implementation of 120 registered projects; and the majority of NGO projects were still not registered with FACS or any part of the central government. Local governmental offices were set up in different parts of Nicaragua to deal with foreign NGOs and solidarity groups in each region.

CONTRIBUTION OF EXTERNAL ASSISTANCE

External development assistance to developing countries is frequently criticized, and often justly. For example, aid can sometimes contribute to massive capital flight. It can be squandered on luxury consumption, especially by the rich, or simply be stolen or disappear through corruption. It can also replace domestic savings, and investments which could have been made without external resources.

In the case of Nicaragua, there was a considerable flight of capital just before, during, and immediately after the revolution. Examination of balance-of-payments accounts and other sources indicates that capital flight since 1980 has been relatively small, and diminishing. The same is true of luxury consumption. The government has increasingly restricted all non-essential imports. Total imports were no higher in 1986 than in 1980. Imports of 'luxury' items have steadily decreased—and have now been practically eliminated. There has also been remarkably little corruption in the use of external or domestic resources in post-revolutionary Nicaragua.

Investment rates in Nicaragua have been high, and large proportions of both external and local resources have been channelled towards reconstruction and development projects. Other criticisms of aid—such as its use for 'show' projects, the way it increases a country's dependency, the wastage it can cause when inefficiently administered, the potential for urban bias and neglect of rural needs, and the possibility that aid merely be a means of financing donor-country exports—apply occasionally to the case of Nicaragua, and are discussed in Part III.

The contribution of aid to social and economic development will be largely determined, however, by the development strategy of the recipient country. The Nicaraguan government has given high priority to meeting the basic needs of the poor majority, increasing popular participation, and building a more autonomous and diversified economy. Notable progress has been made towards these goals despite the dramatic impact of the present war upon the economy and society. By 1987 the war had displaced hundreds of thousands of people and had levied over $1 billion in direct costs. Although the economy has been seriously undermined by the war and the world recession, Nicaragua's growth rates compare favourably with those of most other Central American countries over the 1981-1986 period.

Literacy has dramatically increased, health services have improved, and measures have been taken to guarantee the access to food by large sectors of the low-income population in the midst of critical economic circumstances. Effective popular participation has greatly increased through the growth and influence of UNAG, CST, ATC, AMNLAE and many other mass organizations responsive to the needs and aspirations of different sectors of the population. Progress has also been made in mobilizing domestic resources, transferring technology, strengthening links between agriculture and industry, and diversifying markets and sources of external cooperation, as the chapters in Part III will show. Outside aid has facilitated each of these steps, which together will help establish a more autonomous economy.

WESTERN EUROPEAN AND CANADIAN ASSISTANCE

Assistance to Nicaragua from Western Europe and Canada since the revolution has been both substantial and crucial. Nevertheless, Western assistance may not have been as great as one would expect—judging from the widespread popular sympathy expressed in Europe for the Sandinista revolution. Close ties between more conservative governments in some European countries and the United States have resulted in a restriction of aid to Nicaragua. Changes in their internal political alignments, and budgetary constraints have exacerbated this trend. Nicaragua has furthermore been prevented from becoming a priority recipient for many donors because it is classified by some agencies such as the World Bank as a 'middle-income' country, despite widespread poverty there. As a result, the socialist and social democratic governments in Western Europe and Canada have provided the bulk of concessionary loans, credits and donations; although more conservative governments usually honoured commitments made by their predecessors, and have continued to give substantial indirect aid through government grants to NGOs and contributions to multilateral organizations.

LEVELS OF ASSISTANCE

Official development assistance from just five West European countries (the Netherlands, Sweden, France, Italy and Spain) amounted to $450 million over 1979-85. Other important donors have been Canada, the EEC and, until 1982, West Germany. Half the Central American bilateral and multilateral assistance from the EEC and its member countries went to Nicaragua. According to EEC data, total EEC multilateral aid to Nicaragua exceeded 100 million ECUs between 1979 and 1986, of which over half was food aid. Grants from the EEC, Western European and Canadian governments recorded by the Nicaraguan government averaged about $33 million annually over the same period, although this figure excludes some donations in kind.

After 1980, commitments of new loans and credits from Western Europe and Canada fluctuated greatly. Actual disbursements of official development assistance were much steadier, at about $70 million annually until 1986, when these increased to around $100 million. Commitments of official Western European and Canadian assistance, including donations in kind and aid channelled through the EEC and other multilateral agencies, averaged about $100 million annually. NGO and solidarity-group aid may well have averaged over $30 million a year. Part of this was additional but it also included some official assistance channelled through NGOs. The total of European and Canadian cooperation from all sources amounted to about $120 million annually.

TRADE AND DEVELOPMENT ASSISTANCE

Increased trade accompanied aid from Western Europe and Canada. The total value of Western European and Canadian purchases of Nicaraguan exports has fallen slightly since the late 1970s. Their relative importance to Nicaragua increased sharply, however, as Nicaraguan exports have fallen—especially after 1981. After the revolution, the proportion of Nicaraguan exports to Western Europe and Canada nearly doubled. In 1986, EEC member-country purchases alone accounted for 52 percent of all Nicaragua's exports. Nicaraguan imports from Western Europe and Canada also increased dramatically, doubling from 1978 to 1986.

STABILITY OF AID DISBURSEMENTS

The relative stability in the disbursement of grants, loans and credits from Western Europe and Canada over 1979-85 is principally due to three factors. First, as several countries were involved, any increase or decrease in donations and disbursements from some countries tended to be compensated by others. West Germany was an important donor until 1982, when its Social Democratic government was replaced by a coalition of Christian Democratic and other centrist and right-wing parties. The United Kingdom's Conservative government never provided significant direct assistance but indirectly contributed small amounts through the EEC, various U.N. agencies and some U.K.-based NGOs. Labour or socialist administrations in Spain, Italy, France, the Scandinavian countries and Austria contributed generously, but conservative governments in the same countries later sometimes withheld or reduced assistance. Sweden greatly increased aid in 1985 and subsequent years, adapting it to Nicaragua's changing economic requirements. Switzerland's aid has been relatively steady, reflecting a stable governing coalition and economy. In some countries, however, aid policy and foreign policy have not always been consistent.

A second factor was the stability of certain European and other multilateral contributions to Nicaragua. The EEC has been able to take a more detached view on Central America than many individual governments, which have had to respond to strong conservative forces or U.S. pressures. It has also had huge unmarketable agricultural surpluses which could be disposed of as aid. U.N. agencies such as UNICEF, IFAD, UNDP and WFP have found Nicaraguan development objectives similar to their own, and the Nicaraguan administration of aid to be more honest and cooperative than that of many other developing countries. WFP, for example, could count on its food aid being used for its stated purpose of benefiting low-income consumers. IFAD's aid benefited primarily small peasants and rural landless workers. However, partly owing to U.S. pressure, disbursements of IFAD loans through the Central American Bank for Economic Integration were stopped after 1984.

The third factor enhancing the regularity of assistance to Nicaragua was the desire of West European and Canadian suppliers to fill the trade gap left by the U.S. embargo. There were private profits to be made by these transactions and European suppliers did not want to lose them. At the same time, European public opinion did not endorse U.S. policies in Central America.

The danger now is that with increased budgetary restrictions in Canada and Western Europe, and with more conservative governments in many of these countries, the relative stability in their cooperation up to 1985 may be undermined, and assistance to Nicaragua may dwindle. In 1986, this process seemed already to have begun: while disbursements of old loans and credits increased that year, new commitments fell.

USE OF WESTERN EUROPEAN AND CANADIAN ASSISTANCE

The use made of Western European and Canadian aid followed the trend of overall external assistance: reconstruction and basic needs were the priority in 1979 and 1980, with a shift to large-scale capital-intensive investments after 1980. Countries have tended to concentrate their aid in sectors in which they have specific interests and expertise. Italy's support for geothermal energy development is one example. Canada contributed to the construction of grain storage facilites, a large-scale dairy project and the installation of drinking-water systems. Swedish support was given for mining, forestry and health. The Netherlands concentrated on the port sector, agriculture and health services. Spain provided credits for modern irrigation equipment, and helped finance a huge investment in a modern sugar complex—along with Cuba, several other Latin American countries, Eastern Europe, France, Austria, and Sweden.

With Nicaragua's shift to a survival economy in 1985, and the imposition of the U.S. trade embargo, Sweden, Spain, and France began supplying Nicaragua with essential products it could no longer obtain from the United States (although the French and Spanish credits carried interest rates higher than those Nicaragua was accustomed to paying). Considerable European and Canadian assistance was still committed to large-scale projects, however. Smaller donor countries (Switzerland, Denmark and Norway, the Netherlands, Belgium and Sweden) channelled an important part of their assistance for small projects through NGOs.

THE CRUCIAL ROLE OF NGOS

NGO assistance acts as an important counter-balance to the large-scale projects often favoured by bilateral and multilateral donors, as well as by the Nicaraguan government. Moreover, many of the larger donors lack the personnel or infrastructure to prepare or supervise small-scale initiatives. NGOs have shown that they can fulfill this role—sometimes very effectively. Several Western European governments, the EEC, and Canada appreciate the potential of NGOs and support their own NGOs' activities in Nicaragua. For example, 15 Canadian NGOs alone in Nicaragua receive over half their budgets from the Canadian International Development Agency (CIDA). Half of Swiss bilateral aid has been provided through NGOs. The EEC channelled about $2.6 million through NGOs to Nicaragua in 1986 alone, as a contribution to 39 projects valued at $7.2 million.

The contribution of solidarity committees, volunteer brigades and town-twinning programmes has also been significant. In cities and universities throughout Europe and North America, over 2,000 solidarity committees have played an important political role in informing public opinion about development in Nicaragua and generating support for the Nicaraguan revolution. They organize study tours to Nicaragua and volunteer brigades to help with literacy campaigns, health services, coffee harvesting, and small-scale construction programmes. Participants in these schemes also improve the flow of information from Nicaragua through their personal observations, experiences and contacts. Numerous cities, mostly in Western Europe and Canada but also in the United States, have twinned themselves with a town in Nicaragua. Their contacts and visits also transmit information about contemporary Nicaragua.

FACS administered $4.1 million in NGO aid in 1986, but this was only a fraction of all NGO aid. As an illustration, in 1979-85, NGO aid from Switzerland amounted to about $3 million (or half of its bilateral programme), but only one-tenth of this went through FACS. The same seems to be true for NGO aid from other countries. Total NGO aid (including developmental, humanitarian, technical, church, volunteer, and twin-city assistance) may well have averaged $30-50 million annually since 1979. Much of this, but not all, was in addition to officially recorded bilateral and multilateral assistance. The figure includes NGO aid from the United States, Western Europe and Canada. The most important NGO aid has come from West Germany, Canada, the Netherlands, Belgium, the United States, the United Kingdom, France, Switzerland and the Scandinavian countries. Moreover, the volume of such aid seems to have increased.

NGO aid is not without problems. The quality and effectiveness of projects vary widely. There has been a lack of coordination between some NGOs and the government, as well as between themselves, though recently this seems to be improving. Some projects are undertaken principally because an NGO volunteer or staff-person 'liked' a particular community and wanted to help, whereas the real priorities of the local people, or the development strategy for the area, may have been quite different. The Nicaraguan government and mass organizations are now trying to help NGOs identify priorities and coordinate their activities, through FACS and through regional government offices. Even when NGOs have undertaken important programmes in Nicaragua, some have had no permanent on-site staff or representatives. This inhibits the ability to assist the projects they are financing. Also, NGOs may not exploit the full potential funding from their home countries by helping local organizations in Nicaragua submit timely, well-prepared requests. On balance, however, the contribution of NGOs since 1979 has been vital.

Project Implementation

In the seven years after the revolution, annual external assistance to Nicaragua was triple its pre-revolution rate. Donors who had attempted to work in Nicaragua under Somoza were unanimous in believing that their aid was now being much better used. The three biggest problems of the Somoza period were massive corruption, political repression of popular organizations and initiatives, and an almost complete lack of interest on the part of the government in the donors' humanitarian and social objectives.

The donors we spoke to thought corruption since the revolution had been minimal. Popular organizations among the urban and rural poor, women, and minorities were actively encouraged after the revolution, not repressed. The government now shared the humanitarian, social and development goals of the donor organizations. Moreover, it was prepared to take donors' suggestions seriously, and to innovate. Work in Nicaragua since 1979 has been much easier and more satisfying for the representatives of most donor government agencies and NGOs, in spite of the problems caused by the war, economic crisis, and planning limitations.

Donors felt much the same when comparing their efforts in Nicaragua to their experience in most other underdeveloped countries. For example, practically all believed their aid was being used more effectively in post-revolutionary Nicaragua than in neighbouring Honduras, El Salvador or Guatemala. More surprising, was that many donors who had worked extensively in Africa, Asia and other Latin American countries deemed their assistance to be better used in Nicaragua than in these countries.

They were less sanguine, however, in measuring the actual use of their aid in Nicaragua against what they believed was possible, and certain agencies cited cases where aid has been badly used. Many complained about bureaucracy, inexperience and delays. Another common complaint concerned the lack of both unskilled and skilled labour, and material shortages, in part due to the war. The Nicaraguan counterparts have also often left projects as soon as they knew their jobs, either to do military service or to earn more money in the informal or private sectors, or abroad. Donors who praised the government's goals and cooperativeness often spoke less favourably about its efficiency. Also, some NGOs noted that the government's encouragement of grass-roots organizations, which are supposed to be self-reliant and participatory, has paradoxically sometimes resulted in excessive paternalism or development imposed 'from above'.

Of course, a major preoccupation of all donors was the war. Six West European technicians were killed by the Contras in 1986, two others previously, and one from the United States in 1987. There were clear signs of deliberate attacks on foreigners in order to discourage technical assistance. In 1986 the government and donors imposed restrictions on travel by foreign personnel to areas most subject to Contra infiltration. It was also discouraging for many donors to see projects in which they had invested much time, effort and resources—such as a cooperative, school or clinic—destroyed overnight by a Contra attack.

CASE STUDIES

The five projects we studied in detail (see Part III, Chapter 4) were selected to illustrate the experience of project implementation in different sectors. They were:

- a large-scale, capital-intensive, dairy and genetic improvement project, supported by the Canadian government, Inter-American Development Bank, World Food Programme, and to a lesser extent by the Soviet Union and East Germany;
- a small-scale farmers' cooperative enterprise supplying production inputs and consumer goods, supported by the Swedish government and NGOs including the Swedish Cooperative Centre, Oxfam America, Oxfam 'U.K.', and HIVOS of the Netherlands;
- a major school construction project supported by SWISSAID and the Swiss government;
- a pesticide health and safety programme, administered by CARE Nicaragua and supported by Canadian and U.S. NGOs, including the American Friends Service Committee, Catholic Relief Services, CARE USA, Development and Peace of Canada, Oxfam Canada, and the General Mills Corporation;
- a video training and production centre, supported by West European and North American NGOs, including Oxfam 'U.K.', Christian Aid, the Catholic Fund for Overseas Development, Trocaire, Evangelisches Missionswerk, CEBEMO, Vastenaktie, Oxfam Belgium, Development and Peace of Canada, Oxfam Canada, Interpares, United Church of Canada, the U.S. National Council of Churches, and the United Methodist Church.

The principal problems found in implementing these projects varied considerably according to the nature, size, and location of each project. Most problems concerned shortages of materials and labour, limitations in construction capacity, problems of administration and coordination, and inflation. However, despite the difficulties, we found on balance that the projects have made a positive contribution to development, and have increased people's capacity to survive the effects of acute economic crisis and war.

NOTES

1. *Barricada*, 27, 28 and 29 June, 1987.

PART III:

THE WESTERN CONTRIBUTION TO DEVELOPMENT AND SURVIVAL IN NICARAGUA

1 THE EVOLUTION OF NICARAGUAN DEVELOPMENT POLICY[1]

It is necessary to understand the phases through which Nicaraguan development policy has evolved and the reasons which underlie its evolution, before considering the role of external assistance in Nicaragua's development. This chapter outlines three phases: the first, laying the foundations for development (1979-81); the second, expanding the productive base of the economy (1982-84); and the third, adjusting to a survival economy (1985—). But the historical background to the revolution, and the consequent development model, should be outlined first.

BACKGROUND

At the time of the triumph of the Sandinista-led popular revolution in mid-1979, Nicaragua was an underdeveloped country with less than 3 million inhabitants. Its economy depended on the export of agricultural products, especially coffee, cotton, beef, and sugar; and on producing 'basic grains' (corn, beans, rice and sorghum) for internal consumption.

Roughly half the population was rural: mainly small peasant families with insecure land tenure, who produced basic grains and some livestock. Many worked as part-time labourers. There was also a significant number of full-time labourers, primarily in agro-export production. Nearly 40 percent of the national labour force was engaged in 'services'—for the most part with low and uncertain incomes in the 'informal' urban sector.

There was little industry, and what there was was mostly centred on food-processing and other agro-export related activities. All industry, including construction, mining and timber production, only employed 15 percent of the work force and accounted for only 30 percent of gross domestic product (GDP). There was some textile manufacture (using imported raw materials, not Nicaraguan cotton, which was exported) and production of chemicals and metal goods. Manufacturing was highly dependent on imported technology and raw materials.

The food consumption of the low-income majority was well below minimum standards for health and adequate nutrition. Over half the country's children suffered from under-nutrition and about 15 percent were seriously malnourished. The severest poverty and malnutrition were found in rural areas. Infant mortality rates and health conditions were among the worst in Latin America. Most people had no sanitary facilities or access to safe drinking water. The majority was illiterate and there were few schools in rural areas.

Housing was abysmal. Over half Managua's 700,000 people lived in crude shelters, where they had stayed since the 1972 earthquake which devastated the city, killed nearly 20,000 people, and left most of the survivors homeless. The Somoza government had done virtually nothing to repair the damage, and had largely expropriated for its own purposes the generous international aid after the earthquake. In the mid-1970s over half the country's population was estimated to be living in serious poverty.

A small group of wealthy property owners, agro-exporters, importers, businessmen, financiers, military officers and civilian bureaucrats closely associated with the Somoza family controlled much of the country's wealth, together with most of its exports, imports, finances and the government itself. Many members of the old land-owning and commercial oligarchy had been shunted aside by Somoza's associates. There was an increasingly important middle group of professionals, technicians, merchants and administrators which provided services for the agro-export economy. Middle-sized farmers and ranchers were also relatively numerous, compared with other Central American countries such as El Salvador and Guatemala—where land ownership was more polarized between small peasant producers and large estate owners.

The Somoza family dictatorship exercised power ruthlessly for over 40 years after the withdrawal of the U.S. marines in 1933 and the assassination of General Augusto Sandino in 1934. Discontent, whether latent or overt, had always been widespread. It grew rapidly when the world recession of the late 1970s badly cut export earnings. The Sandinista National Liberation Front (FSLN), founded in 1961, had been mobilizing political support in both rural and urban areas and carrying out guerilla actions against the National Guard. In July 1979, popular insurrections in the major towns and cities culminated in the defeat of the National Guard, and the fall of the Somoza government. The FSLN was clearly the dominant political and military force in the country, although the new National Junta for Reconstruction included many other groups which had collaborated in overthrowing the dictator.

The extensive fighting during 1978 and early 1979 badly damaged the country's infrastructure, especially transport. Nicaragua was heavily indebted to foreign banks and governments. Its GNP fell by one-third between 1977 and 1979. The economy was extremely dependent on foreign technology, markets, inputs and consumer goods—directly or indirectly of U.S. origin. This was in part a heritage of Nicaragua's almost continuous occupation by the U.S. marines (1909-1933) and the subsequent rule of the Somoza family, through its control of the National Guard which the United States had created to 'protect democracy'. Voting, however, was a mere formality with no meaningful choice. Protests or strikes by workers, peasants, students and others were brutally repressed. The country's leading conservative opposition leader and newspaper editor had been assassinated in early 1978. In a word, the new government inherited a devastated and bankrupt country, devoid of democratic practices.

THE NEW DEVELOPMENT MODEL

The FSLN was committed to the profound transformation of Nicaraguan society. Its leaders came from diverse social backgrounds. Some were from middle-class families which had suffered under Somoza and were appalled by the dreadful social conditions and economic dependency of their country; others were from worker, artisan and peasant backgrounds. Some were priests—or deeply religious—and greatly influenced by liberation theology. Others were self-avowed humanists or Marxists.[2] They were united, however, in their rejection of Somoza's rule and the type of dependent capitalist development that had been taking place, and in their determination to bring about a more just society which would meet people's basic needs and be more independent from foreign domination.

On seizing power, the Sandinista government embarked on an ambitious project of reconstruction and development in order to overcome the destruction of the war and the mass poverty left by over four decades of dictatorship. Development required major socio-economic and political transformation affecting the distribution of income, wealth and power; a rapid process of capital accumulation to expand the productive base of the economy; and a new relationship with the world economy.

The principles of autonomous development and non-alignment were central to the revolution. They were the expression of a long-standing opposition to U.S. economic and geo-political domination, and of a need to reduce the vulnerability of the economy to fluctuations in international and U.S. markets. The government therefore sought to strengthen and develop new economic and political ties with a broad range of Western, socialist bloc and Third World countries. In the Constitution approved by the National Assembly in September 1986, this is ratified as a principle:

> "Nicaragua bases its international relations on the principle of non-alignment, in the search for peace, and respect for the sovereignty of all nations. Hence, Nicaragua opposes any form of discrimination; is anticolonialist, anti-imperialist, antiracist and rejects all forms of subordination of one State by another." (Article V)

The fundamental principles of Nicaraguan development policy are to satisfy basic needs, increase popular participation, ensure a mixed economy, and assert self-determination. The term 'mixed economy' in Nicaragua refers to the coexistence of diverse forms of public and private property, but with the state playing a significant role in regulating the allocation of resources, in response to national priorities associated with defence, investment and basic needs. Numerous mass organizations participate in defining these priorites, representing industrial workers (CST), agricultural labourers (ATC), women (AMNLAE), youth (JS19J), agricultural producers (UNAG), and local community residents (CDS).

Nicaraguan economic and development policies have been shaped by pragmatic concerns. A recent Norwegian report on Nicaragua argues that the new government considered the mixed economy, for instance, to be

> "... the only solution which could satisfy the demands for both private sector profits and social redistribution of the country's economic resources. Without a profit incentive, the private sector would have no interest in contributing in the development process, and private sector cooperation was considered absolutely necessary."[3]

Since then, the commitment to a mixed economy has been affirmed in the Nicaraguan Constitution:

> "The mixed economy ensures the existence of distinct forms of property, both public and private, as well as associative, cooperative and communal forms. All these forms of property will contribute towards the superior interests of the Nation and to the creation of wealth for the satisfaction of the needs of the country and its inhabitants." (Article V)

The U.S. Treasury Department has maintained that the "macroeconomic policies of Nicaragua are not propitious for the economic development of the country."[4] However, many European agencies view these policies as consistent with their own definitions of development: not only as economic growth, but as the satisfaction of basic needs, eradication of poverty, and endogenous development.[5] Similar concerns can be found in the charters of many non-governmental development organizations, and in the development policy of the EEC which furthermore upholds the "right of each State to determine its own political, social, cultural, and economic policy options."[6] There has been widespread recognition in Europe of both the Nicaraguan commitment to meeting the basic needs of the majority, and Nicaragua's progress in literacy, health, education, and land reform.

The principles of autonomous development, non-alignment, and a mixed economy have been constantly maintained since the revolution, but there have been three distinct phases of development strategy. During the first phase (1979-81), major emphasis was placed on the reconstruction of economic infrastructure and on meeting some of the long-neglected social and economic needs of the poorer majority of the population. In the second phase (1982-84), a high priority was placed on medium and long-term investments to expand the economy's productive capacity, while at the same time maintaining the levels of social expenditure and investment achieved after 1979. In 1985, however, a third phase with a survival strategy more adapted to conditions of war and crisis was induced by the combined effect of escalating Contra aggression, the U.S. economic blockade, futher deterioration in the terms of external trade, planning problems, and changing social forces. This phase is likely to continue until U.S. aggression ceases or is greatly slowed.

PHASE I: LAYING FOUNDATIONS FOR DEVELOPMENT (1979-1981)

After the revolution, the government gave priority to rebuilding the war-torn economy, expanding social services, and creating an adequate state apparatus to implement a new development strategy. GNP had fallen by one-third during the revolution. Workers, peasants, the unemployed and partially employed, who had supported the revolution, and been crucial in the final insurrection, were demanding benefits. Many of the middle classes, too, were determined to eliminate illiteracy and appalling housing and health conditions. This could not be achieved under the former state apparatus, which had primarily served the interests of the ruling clique. A new and strengthened state structure was needed to meet these demands, and to cope with problems arising from the massive exodus of Somoza supporters, the confiscation of their property and the nationalization of banks and much of foreign trade.

There were numerous accomplishments in 1979-81. Infrastructure destroyed during the war was rebuilt. Major projects and programmes in health, education and social and economic infrastructure were implemented, including the construction of hospitals, health centres, the National Literacy Campaign, housing, the first road linking the Pacific and the Atlantic coasts, and expansion of water and electricity services. New markets in Managua, and the CONARCA programme to eradicate coffee rust disease, were completed. Large quantities of agricultural machinery, industrial equipment and vehicles were imported to replace those destroyed during the war. Many new state institutions were created to enable the new government to plan and regulate the economy.

The expansion of health and education services during this period was spectacular. The number of teachers grew by two-thirds, from 14,209 in 1978 to 24,638 in 1983. The number of health centres increased by over 1,000 percent, from 43 to 532 over the same period. The literacy campaign of 1980, which mobilized 85,000 students and volunteer teachers for a period of five months, brought basic reading and writing skills to hundreds of thousands of people and sharply reduced the official illiteracy rate, from 50 percent to just 12 percent. Housing programmes were also expanded to deal with the critical situation created by the 1972 earthquake and the 1978-79 war, which together had left an estimated 200,000 families homeless. Between July 1979 and July 1983, some 43,000 houses were built in Managua alone.[7] The basic features of a modern state apparatus and a defence system, using both a regular army and popular militias, also took shape during this period.

Foreign credits and donations helped make these improvements possible, in spite of declining export revenues and increasing balance-of-payments deficits. The $1.6 billion external debt left by the Somoza government was renegotiated on generally favourable terms. By the end of 1981, the new government had obtained another $1 billion in external credits, plus $200 million in official donations.

However, there were also numerous difficulties and inefficiencies during this initial period. Capital flight was substantial, especially in 1979 and 1980. National planning was embryonic and partly ineffective, since each ministry and agency was setting its own priorities. Consumer subsidies became increasingly burdensome and much credit was inefficiently used. The import of 'luxury' items continued to be a drain on foreign exchange.

PHASE II: EXPANDING THE ECONOMY'S PRODUCTIVE BASE (1982-1984)

During the 1982-84 period, emphasis shifted from reconstruction to expansion of the productive base of the economy. Increasing resources were also needed for defence, in the face of incursions by the Contra rebels and the menace of a U.S. invasion.

The planning of the investment programme was improved by defining clear objectives: to promote self-sufficiency, guarantee defence, and reduce the balance-of-payments deficit.[8] These included an increase in exports, and the substitution of imports by locally manufactured products; the replacement and expansion of installed capacity; the development and conservation of the country's natural resources, and a determination to rely on these resources for future growth; and the development of existing labour resources.

The development strategy called for major investments in agriculture, agro-industry, and alternative sources of energy. The industrial transformation of the country's natural resources was seen as central to development, linking agriculture and industry, adding value to raw materials, increasing or saving foreign exchange, and promoting a new economic relationship with the rest of the world. Nicaragua sought to reduce dependence on exports of unprocessed raw materials, and those imports of manufactures or processed food products (like cotton thread, canned fruit, and vegetable products) which could be produced domestically with local raw materials. Investments in large-scale geothermal and hydro-electric energy projects were made to reduce dependence on petroleum imports—which accounted for 17 percent of the total import bill during 1981-83.

Major projects were initiated in sugar refining, intensive dairy and tobacco production, vegetable and fruit processing, and African Palm plantations. Several integrated rural development projects, associated primarily with the cooperative sector, were also implemented in some of the more marginal areas of the country. By the end of 1984, 30 large agricultural and agro-industrial projects were under way. The proportion of agricultural investment in relation to total public investment increased from 12 percent in 1980 to 50 percent in 1985. The value of imported capital goods for agriculture and agro-industry averaged $54 million, compared with only $10.4 million a year in 1970-78.

This increase in capital investment distinguishes Nicaragua from the other countries of the region. Whereas in the other Central American countries investment generally fell during the early 1980s, in response to economic recession, Nicaragua alone sustained high rates of accumulation (see Table 1). This contrast was particularly evident in agriculture. In Guatemala and Costa Rica, imports of capital goods to agriculture fell from approximately $36 to $12 million between 1978 and 1982, while in Nicaragua they increased from $13 to $45 million. At over 20 percent of GDP between 1981 and 1984, Nicaragua's capital goods imports in relation to total output were the highest in Central America.

Foreign loans, credits and grants played a crucial role in supporting this ambitious investment programme. The external debt increased from a little over $2 billion in 1981 to nearly $4 billion by the end of 1984 (see Table 2). Official donations amounted to another $250 million (see Chapter 2).

Dependence on external resources had already been deeply ingrained before the revolution with the development of the agro-export economic model. Nicaragua had supplied raw materials to the processing plants of the United States, Western Europe and Japan. Like other Central American economies, Nicaragua was also structurally dependent on the West—both for foreign exchange, and for imports of manufactured products. This outward orientation had hindered the development of an indigenous industrial base which could produce material inputs to production, spare parts, and machinery for internal use. The small Nicaraguan market made manufacturing investment unattractive to foreign companies.

The post-revolutionary government, like its predecessor, had therefore to import the manufactured products it needed. Food imports also rose sharply after the revolution, because though the Sandinistas had redistributed income, they could not satisfy the ensuing demand for basic foodstuffs. Total imports increased considerably and averaged $866 million per year between 1980 and 1986, compared with $593 million between 1974 and 1977. After 1981, imports fell slightly, as most non-essential items were excluded.

Even though imports were held down, the country's capacity to pay for them was declining. Export revenues fell sharply, from $500 million in 1981 to $431 million in 1983, and only $223 million in 1986 (see Table 3). This was partly due to the decline in the world price of sugar, cotton, and sesame seed. The volume of exports of major products like cotton, coffee, beef, seafood, timber and gold also fell for various reasons. Much of the cattle and coffee production, forestry and mining activities was situated in the war zones. The fishing industry on the Atlantic Coast was also seriously affected by the war. Additionally, many private producers of cotton and cattle reduced cultivated areas and the size of herds in response to low prices, to the redistributional measures taken after the revolution, and to their loss of political influence.

Nicaragua's terms of trade deteriorated considerably in this period, as the following examples show:

- An imported jeep cost 33 quintals of coffee in 1977 (1 quintal equals 100 lbs/45.4 kg), but 80 quintals in 1984.
- A tractor cost 106 quintals of cotton in 1974, but 301 quintals in 1984.
- A barrel of crude oil cost 1 quintal of sugar in 1974, but 50 quintals in 1984.

As more and more resources were channelled towards large-scale development projects, difficult choices had to be made between investment and consumption. Imports of consumer goods competed with those of capital goods. Between 1980 and 1984, capital goods destined for industry and agro-industry increased their share from 7 percent to 18 percent of total imports, whereas the share of non-durable consumer goods declined from 24 percent to 13 percent. Shortages of basic consumer goods became increasingly troublesome from 1982 onwards.

In order to finance investment as well as social programmes, and subsidies for basic food products and public transport, government expenditure increased rapidly—and contributed to the growing fiscal deficit. As multilateral sources of international cooperation—especially the World Bank and the Inter-American Development Bank—restricted or suspended loans to Nicaragua, the government was obliged to provide additional finance so that projects could go ahead. Directing so many resources towards large-scale, slow-yielding projects had inflationary consequences: no goods were being produced, but money was being poured into investments.

Investment resources also tended to be concentrated in state enterprises, without necessarily involving the peasantry or private sectors. As the Minister of Agricultural Development and Agrarian Reform explained to delegates at the First National Congress of the Peasantry held in April 1986:

> "We began to execute many projects, and—given our desire to increase production rapidly, and our involvement in land redistribution, we were not able to link the investment programme to the peasant movement or the sector of small- and medium-sized ranchers, who are still waiting for the Revolutionary Government and the Ministry of Agricultural Development to design a comprehensive investment programme for their benefit. Considerable resources were channelled towards high-technology and irrigation projects, while the peasantry did not receive the same treatment."[9]

Production also fell when after the revolution, coercive and paternalistic forms of labour exploitation were eliminated, and the intensity of labour and the length of the working day reduced. Industrial productivity was also badly affected by the foreign exchange crisis, which restricted imports of spare parts and raw materials, creating shortages and considerably disrupting the manufacturing process. Both in agriculture and industry, productivity was also hampered by poor organization of labour, in part caused by the inexperience of the new administrators and planners.

PHASE III: ADJUSTING TO A SURVIVAL ECONOMY (1985—)

The 1985-86 period marked the transition to a 'survival economy'. By mid-1986 some 5,000 Nicaraguans had been killed and another 6,000 wounded by the Contras. But the full human cost of the war was even higher. Around 250,000 people (17 percent of the rural population) had been forced to abandon their homes, and living standards for much of the rural population steadily deteriorated, as access to social services and basic goods declined. Between 1980 and 1985 Contra attacks destroyed 20 health centres. Another 99 had to be abandoned; 48 schools were destroyed and another 502 closed; 840 adult education groups were disbanded.[10] Nurseries, homes, cooperatives and storage facilities for basic food products were also targets of Contra attacks.

The economic and human costs of the war had already begun to rise sharply in Phase II. Economic sabotage by the Contras brought the cost of the war in 1983 to $240 million, compared with $70 million in 1982. Destruction of machinery, equipment and infrastructure, production losses, and restrictions on external credits continued to increase, and more trade was lost: this cost over $300 million in 1984. There was a slight improvement in 1985 as the Sandinistas gained the upper hand in the conflict (see Table 4), but by May 1986 the total economic cost of the war due to material losses, lost credit and trade amounted to over $1 billion—roughly the equivalent of four years' export revenues.[11]

As the war escalated, defence expenditure took up an increasingly large share of the budget, growing from 7 percent in 1981 to 19 percent in 1985. Not only did this constrain other government expenditure, but—above all—it contributed to spiralling inflation, as money supply rose rapidly to cover the fiscal deficit, while production stagnated or fell. The conscription of some 70,000 men into the army by 1984 worsened the already serious labour shortages in agriculture and industry. Resources of manpower and building materials were intolerably strained. The country could not maintain its past rate of investment and still wage a war, even though most of the foreign exchange costs of the investment programme were being financed by foreign grants and credits.

All these factors forced the government to rethink economic policy, as Nicaragua attempted to channel massive resources into the war effort and development projects; and simultaneously to guarantee the domestic supply of basic goods and social services. In practice, this meant a number of important policy changes. First, the minimal requirements of those people engaged in defence and production had to be assured—which meant attempts to satisfy the basic needs of all of the people had to take second place. Second, the slow-yielding, large-scale investment projects had to slow down in order to free more resources for immediate production and consumption. Third, more emphasis had to be placed on stimulating production and investment in both peasant and private sectors.

Many of these changes were initiated in February 1985, with a package of economic measures to permit adjustment to external restrictions, the demands of war, and imbalances in planning. Subsidies were reduced, the currency was devalued, and priorities were established for investment projects. Government employment and expenditure for purposes other then defence were frozen. Incentives were introduced for industrial workers, and significant wage increases given to working-class and state employees. Major efforts were made to stimulate food production by peasants and other producers: producer prices were raised and the land-redistribution programme—which had already been stepped up in 1984—was further accelerated.

The 1986 economic plan carried these measures further.[12] Investment in a number of major projects was curtailed. Efficient use of existing capacity took priority over expansion and new projects. The repair and maintenance of equipment which had deteriorated rapidly over the years received special attention. The drive to boost domestic production continued with several new initiatives. Land redistribution continued, as generous exemption criteria in the 1981 Agrarian Reform Law were eliminated in early 1986. Moreover, by the end of 1986, 40 percent of the land in state farms created out of Somoza's confiscated property had been assigned to cooperatives and individual peasants. Over half of Nicaragua's rural families had received land under the agrarian reform by the end of 1986.

Furthermore, state agricultural and agro-industrial enterprises were expected to provide support services to all types of producers in the area where they operated. Institutions and enterprises were also encouraged to produce their own beans and corn, as was the army, in order to reduce the defence budget and relieve pressure on civilian food supplies. Finally, measures were taken to reduce the fiscal deficit. Some government programmes were cut or frozen, and tax revenues from domestic sources increased, although the practical limits of raising more income from taxes were being rapidly approached.

These measures helped to stimulate basic grain production, control distribution of certain basic manufactured goods, reduce the fiscal deficit as a proportion of GDP, and halt the post-1983 trend of negative growth rates (see Table 5). Less progress was made in other areas, however. Shortages of many basic goods worsened. Above all, the economic measures could not contain inflation, parallel markets, and the growth of the urban 'informal sector'. Inflation, according to the consumer price index, rose from 50 percent in 1984, to 334 percent in 1985 and reached 747 percent in 1986.

In late 1986, the consolidation of a survival economy was still a long way off.[13] Government leaders stressed the need to rely more on domestic resources:

> "the truth of the matter is that the possibility of dealing with our economic problems depends on our ability to mobilize, first and foremost, our own energies and resources."

> "It is true that we receive considerable international cooperation from many countries in the world, but this is not sufficient. Moreover, we cannot continue to think that we can just go on living off foreign aid. International aid should be thought of in terms of a work instrument which, when combined with the efforts, energies and discipline of the people, will generate more production and resources, even in the midst of a war".[14]

> "The defence of the revolutionary state demands that all necessary steps be taken to face and control the crisis, using our own resources and also making the best use of resources from abroad. ...the steps [include]: a more rational distribution and use of resources and better organization in directing the economy, in governmental activity, in political leadership and productive activity; greater discipline, conservation of resources, efficiency, and unity and coherence in carrying out policy."[15]

These priorities, difficulties, and changes in Nicaraguan development policy provide the framework for the following chapters' analysis of the role of international cooperation.

NOTES TO CHAPTER 1

1. This chapter draws heavily on a forthcoming United Nations University publication by S. Barraclough and P. Utting, entitled, "Transition and Development in Nicaragua: Promise, Reality and Prospects".

2. See especially D. Nolan, *La Ideología Sandinista y la Revolución Nicaragüense*, Ediciones 29, Barcelona, 1986.

3. N. Haugstveit, "The Nicaraguan Development Process 1979-85: Conflicts and Constraints", *PRIO Report 2/87*, Oslo, 1987, p. 47.

4. *The New York Times*, 30 June, 1983; quoted in P. Kornbluh, *Nicaragua: The Price of Intervention*, Institute for Policy Studies, Washington D.C., 1987, p. 108.

5. See The Dag Hammarskjöld Foundation, "What Now: Another Development", *Development Dialogue*, no. 1/2, Uppsala, July 1975.

6. *The Courier*, "Third ACP—EEC Convention Signed on 8 December 1984", January-February 1985, Chapter 1, Article 2 (see also Articles 4 and 5).

7. See Instituto de Información de Centroamerica y del Caribe, *The Dawning of Nicaragua*, Managua, 1983.

8. CIERA, "La Capacidad de Gestión del Estado en la Ejecución de Proyectos y Programas Alimentarios-Nutricionales", mimeo, 1986.

9. J. Wheelock, "Balance y Perspectivas de las Políticas de la Revolución en el Campo", *Líneas Para el Fortalecimiento de la Alianza con el Campesinado*, DAP-FSLN, Managua, 1986, p. 22, (authors' translation).

10. Cited in R. Vergara et.al., "Nicaragua: País Sitiado", *Cuadernos de Pensamiento Propio*, CRIES, Managua, 1986, p. 55.

11. R. Delgado, "Nicaragua: Los Costos Económicos de la Agresión del Gobierno de los Estados Unidos de Norte America", paper presented to the 1986 Annual Congress of Nicaraguan Social Scientists, Managua, pp. 10 and 24.

12. See Dirección de Información y Prensa de la Presidencia de la República de Nicaragua, *Líneas del Plan Técnico-Económico 1986*, Managua, 1986.

13. See *ENVIO*, "Slow Motion Towards a Survival Economy", September 1986.

14. President Ortega quoted in *Barricada*, 18 June, 1986, p. 3, (authors' translation).

15. Communiqué of the Extraordinary Session of the Sandinista Assembly, September 1986, (authors' translation).

TABLE 1

INVESTMENT IN CENTRAL AMERICA, 1977-84

(Investment as a percentage of GDP)

Country	1977	1978	1979	1980	1981	1982	1983	1984*
Nicaragua	25.5	11.7	-6.9	16.8	24.6	20.5	21.4	20.1
Costa Rica	28.0	26.3	27.4	29.0	18.4	14.8	18.1	19.6
Honduras	18.2	26.9	26.7	29.1	23.7	15.9	17.2	19.5
El Salvador	24.4	23.6	18.5	13.8	14.5	13.0	13.4	14.2
Guatemala	17.1	18.0	14.9	12.2	14.0	11.8	10.0	10.0

* Preliminary figures.

Source: ECLAC.

TABLE 2

EVOLUTION OF NICARAGUA'S PUBLIC DEBT, 1978, 1980-85

(millions of US dollars and percent)

	1978	1980	1981	1982	1983	1984	1985	1986*
Public debt	961	1588	2200	2730	3324	3900	4370	5260
Debt service ratio**	9.3	17.8	22.3	32.2	14.3	11.7	13.0	25.8

* Provisional figures.

** Ratio of total interest payments to exports of goods and services (percent).

Source: ECLAC.

TABLE 3

EVOLUTION OF TRADE DEFICIT, 1974-77, 1980-86

(millions of US dollars)

	1974-77*	1980	1981	1982	1983	1984	1985	1986**
Imports (CIF)	593.2	887.2	999.4	775.5	806.9	826.2	892.3	880.0
Exports (FOB)	483.7	451.0	499.8	405.8	431.3	384.8	298.5	223.0
Deficit	**109.5**	**436.2**	**499.6**	**369.7**	**375.6**	**441.4**	**593.8**	**657.0**

*Yearly average.

** Preliminary figures.

Source: Ministry of External Trade.

TABLE 4

DIRECT ECONOMIC COST OF THE WAR, 1980-85

(millions of US dollars)

Concept	1980	1981	1982	1983	1984	1985	Total
Material destruction	0.6	4.0	11.0	58.6	27.6	18.3	120.1
Production losses	0.9	3.4	21.1	106.6	170.0	96.4	398.4
Lost external credits	0.0	8.2	38.3	61.3	92.1	73.0	272.9
Losses due to embargo	0.0	0.0	0.0	14.6	16.0	79.4	110.0
Total	**1.5**	**15.6**	**70.4**	**241.1**	**305.7**	**267.1**	**901.4**

Source: Ministry of the Presidency.

TABLE 5

EVOLUTION OF TOTAL GROSS DOMESTIC PRODUCT IN CENTRAL AMERICA

Annual Growth Rate 1981-1986

(percent)

	1981	1982	1983	1984	1985	1986*	Cumulative variation* 1981-86
Nicaragua	5.4	-0.8	4.4	-1.4	-2.6	0.0	5.0
El Salvador	-8.4	-5.7	0.6	1.4	1.4	-0.5	-11.1
Honduras	1.0	-1.6	-0.6	3.1	1.4	2.0	5.5
Guatemala	1.0	-3.4	-2.7	0.0	-0.9	0.0	-6.0
Costa Rica	-2.4	-7.3	2.7	7.9	0.9	3.0	4.0
Latin America**	0.5	-1.4	-2.4	3.2	2.7	3.4	5.9

* Provisional estimates.

** Excluding Cuba.

Source: ECLAC: see publication of United Nations Economic and Social Council, *E/1987/55*, April 1987.

2 THE ROLE OF INTERNATIONAL COOPERATION

Opportunities for international cooperation were numerous after the revolution. This chapter discusses Nicaraguan policies for diversifying and administering foreign aid and trade, and the changing patterns of multilateral and bilateral support from different parts of the world.

The new Nicaragua was able to accommodate many different forms of development assistance from a variety of donors. Aid in the form of emergency relief was used for reconstruction after the revolution, and for the victims of the 1982 floods and the Contra war. The government's large-scale investment projects attracted concessionary loans to support economic growth. Other aid designed to improve the living standards of the poor went to both governmental and community programmes in health, education, housing, welfare, and the provision of drinking water. Numerous initiatives emphasising popular participation drew aid for self-help development and the organization of the poor. Some donor governments and agencies sought to use development assistance as a political lever to constrain the overtly non-aligned stance of the new government. Other more commercially motivated sources provided aid and concessionary credit as a means of creating or expanding their markets in the region. The Nicaraguan government did not, however, accept offers of 'assistance' accompanied by conditions that contradicted the development principles and objectives it had laid down.

The revolution was supported politically not only by progressive parties and governments, but also by more moderate ones: in Europe, North America, Latin America, and elsewhere in the Third World. They saw in Nicaragua the possibility of a 'third way' of development, combining social justice and economic growth with respect for the principles of political pluralism, mixed economy, and non-alignment. Their offers of aid, concessionary loans and credit lines were expressions of their support.

The Nicaraguan government, for its part, had no alternative but to turn abroad for the massive assistance it needed. The country's underdevelopment and external dependence, the deterioration in international terms of trade, the impact of the revolutionary war on production, and capital flight, all combined to restrict the potential for a more self-reliant alternative. As one of the Sandinista leaders explained, "we decided to embark on a rapid and intense reconstruction of the economy which would be costly in terms of the external debt. We should all be clear, therefore, that because of these decisions to import basic goods and other products required for reconstruction, development means more indebtedness now. We have chosen the path of indebtedness in order to be able to invest and improve our situation in the long run, in order to ensure that the standard of living of the people improves and does not deterioriate."[1]

Indeed, the annual debt increased from a 1974-77 average of $171 million, to $537 million between 1980 and 1985. Much of the debt, however, was incurred for investment in agriculture, agro-industry and the energy sector (see Table 6 and Appendix III), which require outside aid in the short and medium term, but contribute to the possibility of a more self-reliant, independent economy in the longer term.

Rescheduling the debt has alleviated its burden on the Nicaraguan economy. The Sandinista government inherited one of the most indebted economies in Latin America with the highest debt in proportion to GDP in the region. Immediately after the revolution, the new government set about renegotiating the $1.6 billion debt left by Somoza. In December 1980, an agreement was reached with private banks to restructure $582 million of the debt. At the same time, bilateral debts were renegotiated—successfully with Spain and West Germany—but not with the United States.

As the internal economic situation deteriorated and foreign exchange became increasingly scarce in mid-1983, Nicaragua decided that debt repayments to the commercial banks should not take precedence over vital economic and social programmes. New negotiations culminated in a short-lived agreement signed in May 1984. Soon after, a third round of negotiations resulted in a new agreement in July 1985.[2] In the same year, an important agreement was signed with the socialist bloc countries in which Nicaragua was able to postpone debt service payments until 1987.

The bilateral loans and credits to Western European countries continued to be repaid when it was clear that new loans would be forthcoming. The Vice-President of the Nicaraguan Central Bank put it like this:

"We are willing to pay and we want to be serious about our international commitments, but we are only going to pay if further loans are forthcoming. In practice, for every dollar that we pay we obtain a loan for five dollars..."[3]

When no new loans were forthcoming from West Germany after 1980, the Sandinistas eventually halted debt service payments to that country. In the words of one analyst of the Nicaraguan debt, "This strategy of renegotiating when possible and repaying when necessary was a pragmatic response to immediate constraints.''[4] As a result of this approach, the amount of foreign exchange allocated to debt servicing declined considerably after 1982. Interest repayments as a percentage of export earnings fell from an average of 24.1 percent between 1980 and 1982, and to 13 percent between 1983 and 1985 (see Table 2).

In order to attract and allocate external resources, the government established the International Reconstruction Fund (FIR) in 1979. The FIR's efforts to encourage international cooperation were backed up abroad by the Nicaraguan diplomatic corps, and a series of trips by high-level government delegations. In March 1980, the Augusto César Sandino Foundation (FACS) was set up, representing 14 trade unions and mass organizations, requesting aid for specific projects from non-governmental, humanitarian and solidarity organizations; assisting the mass organizations in project design and implementation; and overseeing the use of aid. The establishment of these agencies helped bring in large amounts of overseas development aid.

The terms of foreign assistance have been highly concessionary. A considerable proportion has consisted of outright grants from official multilateral and bilateral sources, amounting to about $100 million per year. NGOs provide $30-50 million in grants each year, although a portion of this appears as aid from official sources. Much of the medium and long-term loans and credits carry soft terms, 20-50 year repayment periods, and interest rates of less than 3 percent (see Appendix III). In some cases, the terms of repayment are so concessionary that what are formally classified as loans are virtually donations. Canadian loans, for example, although they may be tied, carry a grace period of 10 years before any payments are due, zero interest, and a 50-year repayment period: thus approximately 95 percent is actually a donation. Medium- and long-term loans and credits have amounted to an average of $495 million per year between 1979 and 1986. Together, these diverse types of cooperation total $4,618 million from 1979 to 1986, or around $600 million annually. These figures are roughly consistent with the growth of Nicaragua's external debt as well as with its balance-of-payments deficit.

Changing Patterns of International Cooperation

The new government's adoption of a non-aligned stance in international relations was accompanied by an explicit decision to diversify its trading partners and sources of external assistance, in order to reduce its vulnerability and especially its dependence on the United States for aid and markets. This aim was largely achieved in the first four years of the Sandinista government, given the variety of governments and international development agencies which were prepared to assist.

The results of this diversification can be seen in Table 7. By 1980 Western Europe was contributing 14 percent of medium- and long-term credits and loans, Latin America 25 percent, socialist bloc countries 10 percent, while the participation of multilateral sources had declined from 78 percent in 1979 to only 36 percent. North American sources contributed 15 percent. African and Asian countries emerged as new sources of development assistance, reaching 14 percent of loans and credits in 1981 (when $100 million came from Libya). Later India gave a $10 million loan, and China $30 million. Of total external resources between 1979 and 1984, 44 percent came from Latin American and Western European countries, and 27 percent from Eastern Europe and other socialist countries.

Trading relations since 1979 have also been radically transformed. The share of foreign trade accounted for by U.S. markets or U.S. companies in Central America has declined, while trade with both EEC and non-EEC countries in Western Europe, and with Eastern Europe, has increased substantially (see Table 8).

The amount of official development assistance received each year appears to have remained fairly stable throughout the post-revolutionary period. Major changes have occurred, however, in the relative contribution of different sources. The most dramatic change has been the drying-up of loans from the United States, and multilateral sources dominated by the United States, as well as of petroleum credits from Venezuela and Mexico. Having contributed over one-third of all new loans granted in 1980, the international and regional financial agencies cancelled all new contracts after 1983. In response to this situation, the Nicaraguan government has had to rely increasingly on socialist bloc assistance.

Here we analyse the changing patterns of international cooperation between 1979 and 1986 according to source: multilateral organizations, including international and regional finance and development agencies, as well as the EEC; bilateral assistance from advanced capitalist and Third World countries; and finally, socialist countries, including the members of COMECON, China and Yugoslavia (see Tables 9 and 10). These changes are illustrated graphically in Chart 1 at the end of the chapter.

MULTILATERAL LENDING INSTITUTIONS

Before the revolution, Somoza's government relied heavily on multilateral credits from agencies such as the Inter-American Development Bank (IDB), the World Bank and the International Monetary Fund (IMF). Since the revolution, relations with these agencies have been subject to considerable tensions, unlike relations with other multilateral institutions such as the EEC, and those within the U.N. system.

The IMF, for example, demanded that the new government immediately repay a $66 million loan granted to the Somoza government just two months before its demise, despite the fact that Somoza took the initial payment of $22 million with him when he left the country. An analyst of the Nicaraguan debt problem notes that

> "relations with the IMF remained businesslike, but the Sandinista government received no financing from this source and showed no interest in accepting the kind of 'conditionality' required for receiving balance of payments support from the IMF. By accepting their international debt obligations and clearing up accounts with the IMF (on loans granted to the Somoza government), the Sandinistas maintained the international respectability that was a necessary condition for receiving new flows of external resources."[5]

Nicaragua's relations with the World Bank and the IDB were quite good in the first two and a half years after the revolution, but subsequently deteriorated. During this initial period the World Bank made substantial loans to Nicaragua, totalling $106.7 million, and the IDB $176 million.[6] In 1982, however, under pressure from the Reagan administration, these two multilateral institutions began an undeclared boycott of Nicaragua. As the United States controls by far the largest share of votes in each bank (35 percent in the IDB and 20 percent in the World Bank), it has been able to exercise considerable influence on the loan approval process. Where it has been unable to veto loans to Nicaragua, the Reagan administration has resorted to other methods of blocking them.

Such actions have been highly controversial, as well as damaging to the two banks' reputations. In their charters, both are committed to assessing loan applications solely on the basis of *economic* considerations. The charter of the IDB expressly prohibits politically motivated decisions: "The Bank, its officers and employees shall not interfere in the political affairs of any member, nor shall they be influenced in their decisions by the political character of the member or members concerned."[7] Latin American and European members of the IDB have protested against Washington's politicization of the Bank on numerous occasions, albeit without success.

In the World Bank, the United States first used its political hand against Nicaragua in February 1982 when an internal Country Program Paper on Nicaragua appeared, recommending drastic cuts in assistance. The report claimed that the 'Marxist-Leninist' approach of the Nicaraguan leaders had alienated the private sector and jeopardized Nicaragua's development prospects.[8] For some, this came as a surprise, since the Bank had published a sympathetic report three months earlier, commending the country's social policies, describing "a very difficult recovery period" facing the country, and concluding that it was "highly desirable" that Nicaragua receive substantial assistance on favourable terms extending into 1984.[9] Based on this assessment, the Bank had prepared to vote on a $16 million loan to finance urban renewal in Managua. The loan was approved in January 1982, with only the United States voting against it.

The Reagan administration later declared that it would oppose any Nicaraguan aid request to any international lending institution.[10] Despite positive technical evaluations of the World Bank's projects in Nicaragua, the country has not received a single new loan since. Nicaragua continued debt service payments to the World Bank until July 1984; payments ceased only when the foreign exchange position worsened and it became clear that no new loans from the World Bank would be forthcoming.

At the IDB, the United States has used primarily contrived technical reasons to obstruct loans to Nicaragua. For instance, in June 1983, it vetoed a loan for a rural roads project, claiming that "the current macroeconomic policies of the Government of Nicaragua are not conducive to economic development". Canadian and Latin American executive directors objected. The representative of Uruguay, Paraguay and Bolivia accused the United States of making decisions "on the basis of political motives in economic disguise".[11]

In another incident a month later, the United States voted against a loan of $628,000 for a furniture-makers' cooperative in Managua. The loan was passed, however, as all the other 42 members of the bank voted for it. Similarly, the United States delayed a $31 million loan for the improvement of Nicaragua's fishing industry numerous times, then insisted on an amendment to require the borrower to guarantee an adequate provision of fuel for the boats. No such clause had ever been attached to any previous IDB fisheries loan, and the move mystified the Board of Directors.[12] The following week, Contra saboteurs blew up the fuel depot in the port of Corinto with the help of the CIA.

Even more offensive to IDB members was the pressure Washington exerted to block a $58 million loan to private farmers requested in 1982. As the United States could not stop approval of the loan once it was presented to the Board of Executive Directors for a vote, it pressurized the Bank's management to keep the loan bogged down in technical committees so that it could not come to the Board for a decision. In addition, the U.S. Executive Director vowed to walk out of any board meeting that considered a loan to Nicaragua, and thus prevent the necessary quorum for a vote to take place.

In January 1985, in an unprecedented move, 25 members of the Bank, representing a voting majority, jointly requested that the loan be placed on the Board's agenda. At this point, the management had to comply. The U.S. Secretary of State George Schultz then personally intervened, with a letter to the president of the IDB, demanding that the loan be blocked.[13] Schultz expressed the U.S. administration's strong opposition to the loan, and implied that the bank would find its U.S. contributions cut off if it approved the loan. In December of that year, a negative technical report on the loan appeared. The loan has yet to be brought to the Board for a vote, and Nicaragua has received no finance from the IDB since September 1983.

In contrast to this experience with the World Bank and the IDB, other multilateral sources less susceptible to U.S. influence have generally maintained their levels of aid to Nicaragua. Donations from U.N. agencies remained constant at around $10 million annually, between 1983 and 1985—which can be explained in large measure by their set criteria for providing aid (see Appendix II). Criteria of need and of government cooperation in the use of aid for its stated purposes were both met in Nicaragua, which meant that programmes like those of UNICEF, UNDP and the World Food Programme were continued and sometimes expanded. EEC aid to Nicaragua was higher in 1985 than in any previous year (see Chapter 3). In 1986, total donations from multilateral sources rose sharply (see Table 9).

Bilateral Development Assistance

The United States

Even before his inauguration in 1981 as President of the United States, Ronald Reagan campaigned to end U.S. aid to Nicaragua. Two days after taking office he suspended the last $15 million instalment of the $75 million in assistance approved by President Carter in 1979. Nicaragua was portrayed as being 'in Soviet hands' and the United States embarked upon a strategy to oust the Sandinistas by exerting economic and military pressure.

In 1981 the United States terminated its financial guarantees for exports to Nicaragua, making corporations reluctant to trade there. In March of the same year, a loan for $10 million to purchase wheat under the PL 480 Program was suspended. The following month all U.S. bilateral aid was suspended indefinitely, including a loan for $11.4 million intended for rural development, education and health programmes. By mid-1981, the CIA was funnelling money to Somoza's National Guardsmen who were carrying out attacks on Nicaragua from Honduras.[14] In 1983, sugar imports from Nicaragua were cut by 90 percent, and a full economic embargo imposed in 1985.

The Nicaraguan government has calculated that by the end of 1985, financial boycotts by the U.S. government and the major multilateral lending agencies had cost $273 million in lost credits (see Table 4, Chapter 1). The total value of projects and programmes affected by financial boycotts amounted to $423 million.[15]

Latin American Countries

Loans and credits from Latin American countries were substantial, and between 1980 and 1984 they amounted to 30 percent of the total. In 1979 and 1980, Mexico, Panama and Venezuela gave generous grants to Nicaragua. Mexico and Venezuela, the largest Latin American contributors, both extended massive petroleum credits under the San José Accord of 1980. This agreement committed them to supplying the five Central American countries with 160,000 barrels of petroleum per day on favourable terms.

In 1982, however, Venezuela suspended petroleum shipments to Nicaragua on the grounds that payment was in arrears. The political nature of the decision was conceded, however, in a statement by an international affairs specialist of the ruling party when he said, "Do you think that Guatemala or Honduras are paying on schedule? No one is paying in Central America, and Nicaragua is being singled out."[16] Mexico then provided the Venezuelan quota as well as its own, until late-1983 when, again on the grounds of insufficient payment, the exports were reduced. In mid-1984, Mexico halted its petroleum supplies altogether, allegedly under pressure from the United States.[17] This forced a fundamental change in Nicaragua's trading relations, since petroleum imports amounted to $145 million a year during 1981-83, or one-sixth of the total value of imports during that period, and over one-quarter of the value of all credits and loans. Other countries such as Brazil, Argentina, and more recently, Peru, have continued to provide assistance.

Socialist Countries

As support was withdrawn by the multilateral banks, Venezuela and Mexico, increasing assistance was provided by the socialist countries. The suspension of the U.S. wheat loan in 1981 was followed by a donation of 20,000 tonnes of wheat from the Soviet Union—which ironically had been originally imported from the United States. After the 90 percent cut in U.S. imports of Nicaraguan sugar, new outlets were found in the Soviet Union, Mexico, Algeria, and Iran. Similarly, significant petroleum shipments from the Soviet Union began only after Mexico's were reduced.

New loans and credits from the socialist countries reached $221 million in 1982. After slight reductions in 1983 and 1984, they increased sharply again in 1985 when the COMECON countries signed new agreements committing $636 million for development projects, petroleum, production inputs, and consumption goods (see Table 10).

In 1985 the socialist bloc and the West European countries tripled their new commitments in response to the U.S. trade embargo. The Nicaraguan President's 13-nation tour of 8 East European countries, France, Spain, Italy, Sweden and Finland in May 1985 (described by the Western media as 'Ortega's trip to Moscow') and the Vice-President's subsequent visit to several West European countries resulted in a net contribution of $400 million, coming equally from East and West European sources.[18] However, new commitments fell back sharply again in 1986, although it is likely that the actual flow remained fairly constant. From 1979 to 1986, socialist bloc assistance averaged 42 percent of the total, but increased from 31 percent in 1981-83 to 68 percent in 1984-86 (see Table 11).

Increased reliance on assistance from the socialist bloc countries had advantages, and disadvantages. One advantage of trade with the COMECON countries and China was cheaper prices for many products. A Russian-made 'Belarus' tractor, for example, costs Nicaragua approximately half as much as a U.S.-made 'John Deere'. After a further increase in trade with China during 1986, the Ministry of Agricultural Development and Agrarian Reform reported that prices (including freight charges) of a range of agricultural implements, were 11 to 52 percent cheaper than competing imports from El Salvador and Spain.

The countries of the socialist bloc have often paid high prices for Nicaraguan exports: sometimes double world market prices. In 1985, for example, when world sugar prices were well below the cost of production in Nicaragua, Cuba agreed to purchase Nicaraguan sugar at a price which covered production costs. Most of these countries, however, required that revenue gained as a result of higher prices be used to cancel debts or to purchase more goods; although some attached no strings. In 1986, higher prices paid by the socialist bloc countries (mainly East Germany, the Soviet Union and Cuba) accounted for an additional $17 million, or 8 percent of total export earnings.

Another advantage has been the willingness of the COMECON countries to adapt trade and development assistance to the changing priorities and requirements of the Nicaraguan government. In particular, their emphasis has shifted away from capital goods imports tied to specific projects, towards increasing imports of 'operational resources', i.e. production inputs, spare parts and consumption goods.

Disadvantages of increased reliance on COMECON markets and lines of credit include higher transport costs: 11,000 km separate Corinto and Leningrad; Nicaragua's major ports are located on the Pacific Coast, so ships from the Soviet Union and Eastern Europe must pass through the Panama Canal, and passage to Central America can take up to a month. Moreover, until recently, trade went largely in one direction, since Eastern Europe was purchasing few Nicaraguan exports.

Easy access to socialist bloc technology meant Nicaragua imported far more vehicles than it was capable of maintaining or repairing, resulting in a rapid deterioration of tractors, cars, trucks, and buses. In a frank assessment of the performance of the agricultural sector in 1986, the Nicaraguan Minister of Agricultural Development and Agrarian Reform admitted that 30 percent of the country's tractors (mainly the Soviet-made 'Belarus' type) were out of order.[19] At the same time, the general policy of trade diversification had led to a significant increase in the number of models and makes of machinery and equipment being used in Nicaragua, which enormously complicated the task of obtaining spare parts and training repair and maintenance personnel and machine operators.

An additional problem with increased trade with the socialist bloc concerned the type of medium-term supply agreements which governed the export of goods to Nicaragua. Such agreements made it difficult to adapt production or investment patterns rapidly to different circumstances, arising, for example, from variations in climatic conditions, or fluctuations in world commodity prices.

Furthermore, contrary to what might be expected, credit terms were often less concessionary than those offered by Western European governments. In 1986, for example, the principal credits from Eastern Europe carried interest rates of 4-5 percent, to be repaid over relatively short periods. On the other hand, as noted above, COMECON countries were prepared to enter into agreements which enabled Nicaragua to postpone repayments or repay part of the debt through preferential pricing agreements for Nicaraguan exports.

The other major disadvantage was, of course, political. The U.S. administration portrayed Nicaragua's closer relations with the socialist bloc as evidence of the Sandinistas' increasing 'communist leanings'. The United States used this argument to increase pressure on multilateral institutions and West European nations to restrict assistance to Nicaragua.

WESTERN EUROPE

Western European governmental and non-governmental (NGO) assistance is analysed in detail in Chapter 3. It is important to note here, however, that Western European governments have followed a very different line from the U.S. Whereas new commitments from the U.S. government and U.S.-dominated multilateral agencies dried up altogether after 1983, the average amount of new Western European loans and credits during the 1984-1985 period actually increased relative to the previous four years.

ADMINISTRATION OF EXTERNAL RESOURCES

In 1979, the government established the International Reconstruction Fund (FIR) to seek, receive and allocate official development assistance. The following year the Augusto César Sandino Foundation (FACS) was set up to seek and oversee the use of NGO aid. A clearer institutional structure to administer external resources emerged in 1981-82, however, when three divisions within the Ministry of Planning (MIPLAN) began jointly to oversee the flow and allocation of aid.[20] The Department of Technical Cooperation (which was subsequently transferred to the FIR) regulated technical assistance, determined which sectors were most in need of technical expertise, and saw that incoming qualified personnel were distributed accordingly. The Department of Socialist Countries, which oversaw financial and commercial relations with the COMECON countries, undertook the first studies to define future areas for cooperation. An inter-ministerial commission, linked to the Department of Investment, evaluated project proposals and attempted to regulate investment to make projects compatible with the government's policy guidelines, and with the actual capacity to implement projects. Despite this allocation of responsibilities, projects were still authorized that were not in strict accordance with priorities or capacities, due to pressure from different ministries, foreign governments and development agencies.

From 1983, FIR attempted to ensure greater compatibility between Western development assistance and the real needs of the economy. Investment was still determined, however, more by the availability of external resources than by the economic plan. In January 1985, after Daniel Ortega took office as President, organizational improvements were made. Certain departments of MIPLAN and the FIR were merged to form the Ministry of External Cooperation, whose specific mandate was to ensure that the different forms of international cooperation were compatible with the needs of the economy, and to acquire the external resources needed.

In recent years, an attempt has also been made to improve the regulation of NGO aid, dispersed over thousands of small-scale projects which were not even considered in the national plan. As the head of FACS explained,

> ''After the revolution international volunteers and aid agency representatives poured into Nicaragua, all eager to undertake projects. In some cases the projects implemented reflected, first and foremost, their own interests and priorities, which were not necessarily those of the Nicaraguan government. Volunteers

might visit a rural community, fall in love with the local people and decide that there they would build something. It was quite possible, however, that neither that community, nor that particular something were what the national or local authorities considered a priority."[21]

During the early 1980s, some NGOs avoided dealing with the FIR and FACS in order to escape bureaucratic delays in project approval and implementation. After a decentralization of the government in 1982, NGOs began to deal directly with the authorities in the regions where the projects were to be located. Serious problems in regulating NGO activities persisted nevertheless.

Since 1985, FACS and the new offices established in the different regions to attract and oversee the use of aid in small projects have attempted to improve coordination with the NGOs, and have done so quite successfully, according to NGO representatives. FACS has defined priorities for project implementation (such as small-scale integrated rural development projects for the cooperatives) and has encouraged NGOs to coordinate their activities in line with these.

However, there is still a long way to go. The Ministry of External Cooperation has not been able to advance as quickly as originally intended in regulating the activities of the NGOs. The late Director of the Matagalpa Regional Office for International Relations and External Cooperation said that while more NGOs were coordinating their activities with the regional authorities, the massive task of registering all projects in the region had only just begun.

ADAPTING EXTERNAL ASSISTANCE TO CHANGING CONDITIONS

As the priorities of the Nicaraguan government have changed with the worsening economic cirsumstances and the war, external assistance has been gradually redirected to support the present survival economy, which needs to sustain the defence effort, produce a minimum of essential goods, and withstand the impact of inflation. Official development assistance from multilateral and bilateral sources has sometimes been difficult to redirect. Western governments and international agencies have generally preferred to fund highly visible investment projects, rather than help with immediate production and the maintenance and repair of existing equipment. Negotiations to redirect external resources towards working capital and consumption goods were at times difficult and slow, particularly when this meant altering the content of agreements already signed.

It was not really until 1986 that Western European countries were prepared to increase concessionary finance for operational costs. The socialist bloc countries were more flexible. Thus Nicaragua has generally obtained more operational resources from the COMECON countries and China, and machinery and equipment for medium-term investment projects from the OECD countries.

Among Western European donors (as will be seen in the next chapter) some countries including Spain, France, and Sweden have adapted relatively quickly to the changed priorities of the Nicaraguan government. They have supplied Nicaragua with key production inputs and consumption goods, many of which have substituted products previously acquired from the United States. While the credits granted by several of these countries to obtain these goods were not as concessionary as those Nicaragua had been accustomed to, they were crucial in mitigating the effects of the U.S. embargo. The obvious irony is that the relative ease with which the Sandinistas were able to avoid dramatic economic disruption was as much due to the support of U.S. allies, and of U.S. transnational corporations in Western Europe, as to COMECON support.

The next chapter takes up Western Europe's role in contributing to Nicaragua's development and survival.

Notes to chapter 2

1. J. Wheelock, *Entre la Crisis y La Agresión: La Reforma Agraria Sandinista*, Editorial Nueva Nicaragua, Managua, 1984, pp. 71-2, (authors' translation).

2. R. Stahler-Sholk,"Foreign Debt and Economic Stabilization Policies in Revolutionary Nicaragua", in R. Spaulding (ed.), *The Political Economy of Revolutionary Nicaragua*, Allen and Unwin, Boston, 1986, p. 160.

3. R. Gutierrez, "Plan Económico 1986", in *Cuadernos de Sociología*, January-April, Escuela de Sociología, Universidad Centroamericana, Managua, 1987, p. 34, (authors' translation).

4. R. Stahler-Sholk, op.cit., p. 165.

5. Ibid., p. 157.

6. "U.S. Overseas Loans and Grants, Obligations and Loan Authorizations, July 1, 1945—September 30, 1985", U.S. Agency for International Development, Washington D.C., 1986, p. 209. The figure includes $37.0 million in soft window loans (IDA), and $69.7 million in hard-window loans (IBRD).

7. Quoted in Center for International Policy, "Redlining Nicaragua", *International Policy Report*, December 1985, p. 2.

8. IBRD, "Country Program Paper: Nicaragua", 16 February, 1982; quoted in J. Kelly and W. Bello, "Banking on El Salvador and Against Nicaragua", *Counterspy*, September-November 1982.

9. IBRD, "Nicaragua: The Challenge of Reconstruction", 9 October, 1981, p. 57.

10. Quoted in J. Kelly and W. Bello, op.cit., pp. 45-46.

11. Document of the IDB, "Minutes of Meeting of the Board of Executive Directors" (DEA 83/21), 22 June, 1983.

12. Letter from Kevin O'Sullivan, IDB staff member, to Hugh Arbuthnot, Esq. (Under Secretary of the International Division at the British Overseas Development Administration), 8 February, 1985.

13. Letter from U.S. Secretary of State, George P. Schultz, to IDB President Ortiz-Mena, 30 January, 1985. See also *Washington Post*, 8 March, 1985.

14. P. Kornbluh, *Nicaragua: The Price of Intervention*, Institute for Policy Studies, Washington D.C., 1987, p. 20.

15. R. Delgado, "Nicaragua: Los Costos Económicos de la Agresión del Gobierno de los Estados Unidos de Norte America", paper presented to the 1986 Annual Congress of Nicaraguan Social Scientists, Managua, see Appendix, Table 4.

16. R. Matthews, "Oil on Troubled Waters", *NACLA: Report on the Americas*, vol. XVIII, no. 4, July/August 1984, New York, p. 39.

17. See P. Kornbluh, op.cit., pp. 116-117, and *International Herald Tribune*, 29-30 September, 1984.

18. D. Siegel and T. Spaulding, *Outcast Among Allies: The International Costs of Reagan's War Against Nicaragua*, Institute for Policy Studies, Washington D.C., 1985, p. 11. See also *Barricada*, May/June 1985.

19. MIDINRA, *Plan de Trabajo 1987: Balance y Perspectivas*, Managua, 1987, p. 29.

20. For a more complete discussion of the institutional organization associated with external cooperation, see M.O. Colin, "La Problemática de la Cooperación Internacional", p. 7-13, paper presented at the 1986 Annual Congress of Nicaraguan Social Scientists, Managua.

21. Interview with the head of FACS, Edwin Zablah, Managua, Autumn 1986.

TABLE 6

AMOUNT AND USE OF EXTERNAL DEBT

	Billions of US $	percent
Accumulated debt:	4.3	100
Pre-revolution (19-7-79)	1.6	37
Post-revolution (1979-84)	2.7	63
Use of New Debt (1979-84):	2.7	100
Investment*	1.0	37
Capitalization of interest	.4	15
Working capital and consumption goods	1.3	48

* Using alternative definitions and criteria, some analysts have estimated that approximately half of total external cooperation has been invested.

Source: Ministry of Planning.

TABLE 7

STRUCTURE OF MEDIUM- AND LONG-TERM LOANS AND CREDITS, 1979-86

(percent)

Source	1979	1980	1981	1982	1983	1984	1985	1986	Total
I. Multilateral	78	36	11	19	16	—	—	—	17
International	8	14	4	8	—	—	—	—	4
Regional	70	22	7	11	16	—	—	—	13
II. Bilateral	22	54	66	36	51	40	16	26	41
Western Europe	6	14	8	8	22	10	14	12	11
North America	—	15	—	—	—	5	1	—	3
Latin America	16	25	44	28	21	25	1	9	23
Africa and Asia	—	—	14	0.6	8	—	—	5	4
III. Socialist	—	10	23	45	33	60	84	74	42
Total	**100**	**100**	**100**	**100**	**100**	**100**	**100**	**100**	**100**

Source: Ministry of External Cooperation.

TABLE 8

STRUCTURE OF FOREIGN TRADE, 1974-77*, 1981-83*, 1985, 1986
(percent)

Economic region	EXPORTS				IMPORTS			
	1974-7	1981-3	1985	1986††	1974-7	1981-3	1985	1986††
I. Developing countries	35.3	26.2	16.6	8.4	43.3	47.4	23.2	23.3
CACM**	22.8	11.6	8.1	5.0	21.6	17.5	6.4	6.1
Latin America†	2.1	2.6	†††	1.1	14.7	25.6	11.4	9.9
Others	10.4	12.0	8.5	2.3	7.0	4.3	5.4	7.3
Caribbean	—	1.7	1.1	—	—	2.9	2.3	4.1
Asia	—	10.3	7.4	—	—	1.5	2.4	2.1
Europe	—	—	—	—	—	—	0.7	1.1

II. OECD members	63.9	65.0	78.1	71.2	56.3	42.5	33.3	25.8
USA	24.8	22.8	6.7	—	28.8	22.0	7.5	0.6
EEC	24.3	22.7	39.6	52.1	14.1	11.7	12.2	17.1
Others	14.8	19.5	31.8	19.1	13.4	8.8	13.6	8.1
III. COMECON countries	0.8	8.7	5.3	20.4	0.3	9.9	42.9	48.0
Eastern Europe	—	6.3	2.5	—	—	6.8	38.0	43.8
Others	—	2.4	2.8	—	—	3.1	4.9	4.2
IV. Others	—	0.1	—	—	0.1	0.2	0.6	2.9
Total	**100**	**100**	**100**	**100**	**100**	**100**	**100**	**100**

* Yearly average.

** Central American Common Market countries.

† Mexico, Panama and South America.

†† Preliminary figures.

††† Insignificant amount.

Source: Ministry of External Trade.

TABLE 9

OFFICIAL GRANTS TO NICARAGUA BY SOURCE, 1979-86
(millions of US dollars)

	1979	1980	1981	1982	1983	1984	1985	1986*	Total
Multilateral	9.4	25.3	9.0	14.1	12.7	19.6	13.3	32.9	136.3
Western bilateral**	73.6	53.9	27.7	22.6	24.0	23.4	19.5	41.3	286.0
Socialist countries	—	0.8	4.5	27.3	40.4	68.4	43.5	72.7	257.6
Total	**83.0**	**80.0**	**41.2**	**64.0**	**77.1**	**111.4**	**76.3**	**146.9**	**679.9**

* The increase in grants reported in 1986 is partially due to improved accounting procedures.

** Includes Western European, Third World and North American countries.

Source: Ministry of External Cooperation.

TABLE 10

MEDIUM- AND LONG-TERM LOANS AND CREDITS, 1979-86

(millions of US dollars)

Source	1979	1980	1981	1982	1983	1984	1985	1986	Total
I. Multilateral	213.0	171.9	86.7	93.6	65.6	—	—	—	630.8
International	22.0	67.0	33.7	37.0	—	—	—	—	159.7
Regional	191.0	104.9	53.0	56.6	65.6	—	—	—	471.1
II. Bilateral	58.7	255.1	495.7	180.2	204.0	135.3	120.0	55.4	1,504.4
Western Europe	14.6	63.6	60.2	38.7	86.7	33.5	106.9	26.0	430.2
North America	—	72.6	—	—	—	15.7*	7.6*	—	95.9
Latin America	44.1	118.9	332.5	138.5	83.5	86.1	5.5	19.4	828.5
Africa and Asia	—	—	103.0	3.0	33.8	—	—	10.0	149.8
III. Socialist	—	45.0	174.9	221.9	132.3	206.4	636.3	160.9	1,577.7
Total	**271.7**	**472.0**	**757.3**	**495.7**	**401.9**	**341.7**	**756.3**	**216.3**	**3,712.9**

* Canadian loans.

Source: Ministry of External Cooperation.

CHART 1

OVERVIEW OF CHANGES IN SOURCES OF DEVELOPMENT ASSISTANCE TO NICARAGUA, 1978-1986

CHART 1—1978*

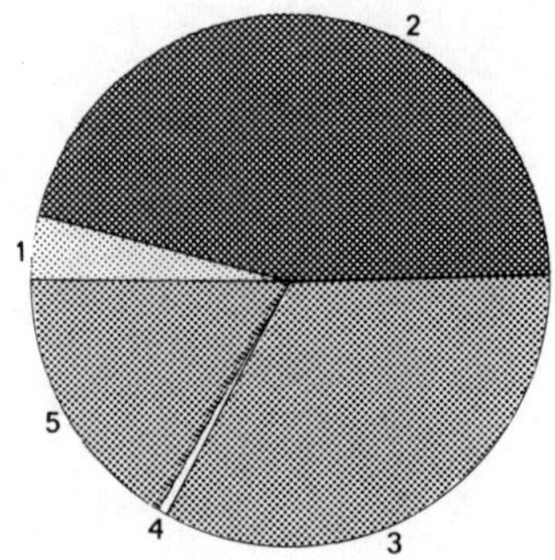

CHART 2—1979-80

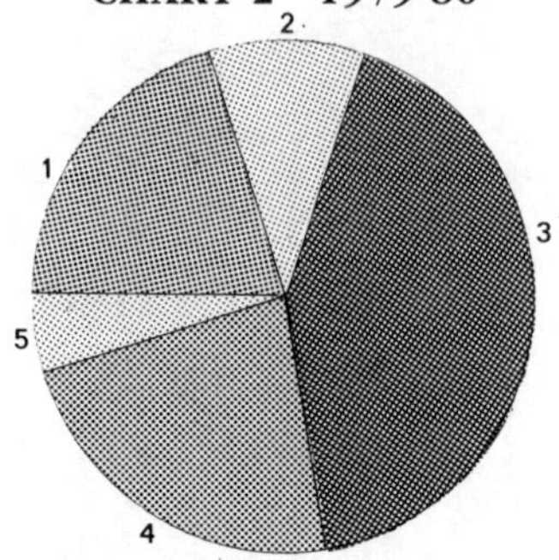

1	WESTERN EUROPE, CANADA 4.2%	WESTERN EUROPE, CANADA, EEC 20%
2	UNITED STATES 45.5%	UNITED STATES 10%
3	MULTILATERAL 33.5%	MULTILATERAL 42.2%
4	JAPAN 0.4%	LATIN AMERICA, ASIA, AFRICA 23%
5	OPEC COUNTRIES 16.4%	SOCIALIST BLOC 4.8%

CHART 3—1981-83

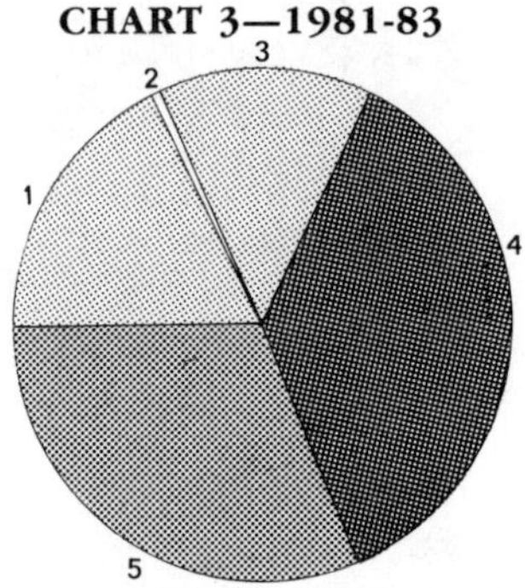

CHART 4—1984-86

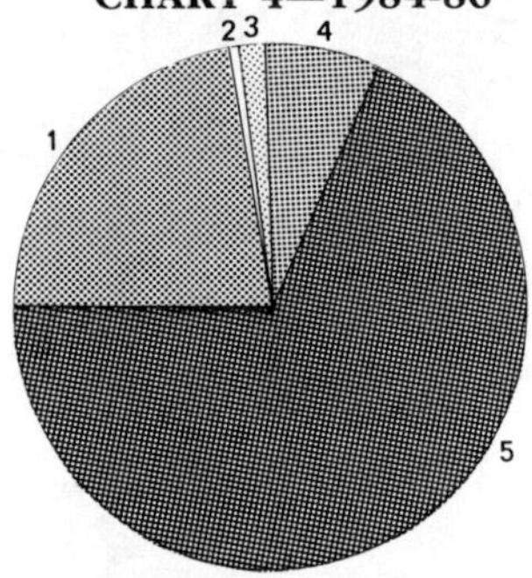

1	WESTERN EUROPE, CANADA, EEC 17.5%	WESTERN EUROPE, CANADA, EEC 22.2%
2	UNITED STATES 0.6%	UNITED STATES 0.5%
3	MULTILATERAL 13.9%	MULTILATERAL 1.7%
4	LATIN AMERICA, ASIA, AFRICA 36.8%	LATIN AMERICA, ASIA, AFRICA 7.3%
5	SOCIALIST BLOC 31.2%	SOCIALIST BLOC 68.3%

Source: See Table 11.

* Includes small amounts from OECD (Japan, Australia, New Zealand), miniscule, however, in comparison with the amounts from less developed countries.

TABLE 11

SOURCES OF MEDIUM- AND LONG-TERM LOANS AND CREDITS AND MULTILATERAL, BILATERAL AND NGO GRANTS

Source	1978 $mn	1978 %	July 1979-80 $mn	July 1979-80 %	1981-83 $mn	1981-83 %	1984-86 $mn	1984-86 %
Western Europe, Canada and EEC	2.5	4.2	190.2	20.0	337.0	17.5	385.5	22.2
United States	26.0	45.5	95.5	10.0	10.7	0.6	7.3	0.5
Multilateral	18.6	33.5	401.9	42.2	268.6	13.9	30.1	1.7
Socialist countries	—	—	45.8	4.8	601.3	31.2	1,188.2*	68.3
Latin America, Asia** and Africa	0.3	0.4	217.9	23.0	708.9†	36.8	127.1	7.3
Others	9.4	16.4***	0.4	0.0	0.7	0.0	0.7††	0.0
Total	**56.8**	**100.0**	**951.7**	**100.0**	**1,927.2**	**100.0**	**1,738.9**	**100.0**

* Includes credits for petroleum imports.

** Includes small amounts of Japanese assistance.

*** OPEC countries in 1978.

† Over half of this amount was accounted for by concessionary petroleum credits from Venezuela and Mexico.

†† Excludes certain grants from Australia.

Source: For 1978: OECD data on disbursements, see *Geographical Distribution of Financial Flows to Developing Countries 1976/1979*. For 1979-1986: based on Ministry of External Cooperation cata for commitments of medium- and long-term loans, credits and official grants; and on TNI estimates of NGO aid.

3 WESTERN EUROPEAN AND CANADIAN ASSISTANCE

The tenor of Western European and Canadian relations with Nicaragua is influenced by both the historical and the recent political context of the Central American region. In particular, bilateral trade and aid with Nicaragua have been heavily affected by changing internal political alignments in these countries, and by the United States' policies towards Nicaragua and its pressure on other governments to support them. Against this, the relative autonomy of many donor countries, and of some multilateral, and many non-governmental organizations stands out.

HISTORICAL CONTEXT

From the Spanish conquest to the beginning of the 20th century, Nicaragua's main commercial and political ties were with Europe. Rival U.S. interests emerged from the 19th century onwards, notably when U.S. filibuster William Walker attempted to make himself President of Nicaragua in the 1850s, but was overthrown by a Central American army. At the time, the Atlantic Coast region of Nicaragua—over half the country's land area—was virtually a British Protectorate under nominal Nicaraguan sovereignty. It remained so for most of the 19th century, until a Liberal government headed by José Santos Zelaya (1893-1909) and backed by a new class of coffee producers and exporters, reasserted Nicaraguan control. The Zelaya government initially enjoyed the support of the United States, which sought to oust European interests from Central America. Relations deteriorated, however, when Zelaya insisted on maintaining free access to European markets and began to negotiate with European financiers to build a trans-isthmus canal as an alternative to the one planned by the United States in Panama. Subsequent military intervention in 1912, lasting two decades, and the war in Europe left the United States dominant, not only militarily, but also economically and politically.

The rapid economic expansion of Western Europe and Japan after World War II sharply altered the picture that had prevailed during the inter-war depression years. While U.S. military dominance remained unquestioned in Central America, its control over the region's trade progressively diminished. In 1950 the United States accounted for over two-thirds of the region's foreign commerce and investments; 70 percent of Nicaraguan exports went to U.S. markets; and U.S. companies furnished

81 percent of Nicaragua's imports. By 1979, however, trade with the United States had fallen to only one-fourth of the total, and a comparable share was directed towards Western Europe and Canada. The Central American Common Market accounted for most of the rest, and trade relations were growing rapidly with other Latin American countries, especially Mexico, Venezuela and Brazil, and with Japan. By 1979, therefore, U.S. commercial hegemony in the region had given way to a predominantly trilateral pattern of trade with the rest of Latin America, Western Europe and the United States; and Japan was rapidly becoming a fourth partner.

Western Europe's markets in Central America, like those of the United States, are only a small fraction of its total foreign trade (less than one percent in both cases). But in the competition for foreign markets and geo-political influence, it has been predictable that there would be contradictions between U.S. and Western European interests in the region.

Recent Political Context

Many Western European and non-aligned nations responded to the Nicaraguan revolution with aid and declarations of solidarity. Even moderate European parties and governments were supportive. When U.S. policy became overtly hostile, many people in Europe disagreed with the perception of the revolution as a threat to U.S. security interests. On the contrary, they saw in Nicaragua a potential 'third way' of development, tied neither to U.S. nor Soviet interests, and coupling economic growth with social justice and political pluralism.

Unlike the Reagan administration which maintains that the source of the turmoil in Central America is the 'incursion of communism' via the Sandinista government, many analysts in Western Europe see extreme social injustice as its root cause. They "question whether every socialist government established in Central America will necessarily be automatically converted into a Soviet ally and a base for sophisticated offensive arms", as has been stated by the director of the Institute for European-Latin American Relations established by the European Parliament.[1]

When the foreign ministers of the EEC member countries met in Costa Rica in 1984, they emphasised the social and economic causes of conflict in the region. They invited the Contadora countries to the meeting to underline European support for negotiated, rather than military, solutions to such conflicts. Furthermore, despite pressure from Washington, they refused to exclude Nicaragua from the regional cooperation agreement, authorizing $45 million in aid. In 1985 the European Parliament described U.S. policy in the region as "in contradiction with the interests of the Central American states".[2] More recently in 1986, the Congress of the Socialist International (SI) condemned "the Reagan administration's policy of destabilization, economic boycott and military assistance to irregular forces which operate against that independent and sovereign nation [Nicaragua]".[3]

When the United States cut off aid and trade with Nicaragua, Western European and other countries helped fill the gap. Multilateral loans to Nicaragua blocked by the United States were in some cases replaced from European sources. The Netherlands and Denmark, for example, provided funds for road construction and drinking-water projects turned down by the Inter-American Development Bank.[4] Although there is no European consensus on Nicaragua, such actions and statements reveal that there are, in the words of a recent Norwegian report, "quite profound differences" between the European and U.S. assessment of the political situation in Central America.[5] The large increase in Western European trade and aid to post-revolutionary Nicaragua should be seen within this context.

TRADE AND OFFICIAL DEVELOPMENT ASSISTANCE

After the overthrow of the Somoza dictatorship, the European response was immediate. The EEC sent emergency food aid valued at over $4 million, and initiated support for longer-term development projects. The SI was particularly active in mobilizing support for the new government. In August 1979 a high-level SI delegation from 14 countries, headed by its Secretary General and Vice-President, visited the war-torn country and appealed to all 'democratic nations' to support Nicaragua with food and medicines. An International Committee for the Defence of the Nicaraguan Revolution was set up by Willy Brandt and presided over by Felipe Gonzalez to mobilize large-scale international material and political support for the revolution.[6] Even conservative governments in Switzerland, Norway and Finland would offer development assistance to Nicaragua. West Germany provided substantial assistance until its change of government in 1982. The bulk of Western concessionary loans and donations to Nicaragua, however, was provided by social democratic governments in the Netherlands, France, Spain,

Sweden and Italy. Official development assistance from these five countries between 1979 and 1985 amounted to approximately $450 million.

West European and Canadian cooperation with Nicaragua since 1979 has, by any measure, been substantial. Total aid can be placed at roughly $120 million annually, although precise quantification is impeded by differences in sources and definitions, and a simple lack of complete data, especially for aid from NGOs and other non-official sources.

GRANTS

Grants from the EEC and from West European and Canadian governments are estimated at around $33 million per year between 1979 and 1986, according to data from the Nicaraguan Ministry of External Cooperation. This figure excludes considerable donations in kind, however, like most EEC food aid—which has been as large as its monetary assistance. The largest grants have come from Sweden, the Netherlands, France and Canada. Canadian aid has fluctuated since 1984, while Switzerland, Norway and Finland have increased aid in recent years. Aid from the EEC increased to nearly 20 million ECUs annually in 1981 and 1982, decreased in the following two years, and rose again to over 20 million ECUs in 1985 (see Table 12).

LOANS AND CREDITS

New bilateral credits from Western Europe and Canada averaged over $50 million annually from 1981 to 1984 and jumped to about $114 million in 1985, falling back sharply again in 1986 (see Table 10, Chapter 2). The increase in 1985 was largely accounted for by new medium-term commercial credits from Spain and France, to help Nicaragua import the equipment and parts needed to keep the economy running, and new credits from Italy in support of geothermal energy development.

Loans, credits and grants (including food aid and other aid in kind) from Western Europe and Canada through bilateral agreements and multilateral and regional organizations have varied from year to year, but remained in excess of $100 million annually from 1980 to 1985.

TRADE

Estimates of trade data with Western Europe and Canada are shown in Table 13. Nicaraguan exports to these countries have amounted to some $150 million dollars annually since 1980. Imports from Western Europe and Canada have increased rapidly, from just over $100 million in 1980, to $210 million in 1986. This reflects the U.S. economic blockade, and increasing trade flows financed by Western European credits and donations. Table 13 shows how the total trade balance has clearly shifted towards this group of countries. In 1979 Nicaragua enjoyed a positive trade balance of $111 million dollars with Western Europe and Canada. By 1981 a deficit was recorded which rose to $62 million by 1986.

U.S. PRESSURES ON EUROPE

Great Britain, with a conservative party in power since 1979, has been the one European country most consistently aligned with the U.S. on Nicaragua since the departure of Somoza. When most European countries protested against the U.S. politicization of the IDB and the World Bank, and their refusal to consider loans to Nicaragua, Britain actively colluded with the United States in concocting technical reasons for objecting to the loans.[7] The British government was moreover the only one in Europe to refuse to send official observers to Nicaragua's 1984 elections.[8] And when Nicaragua charged the United States with the violation of international law at the World Court in the Hague, the British representative was the only European judge to back the U.S. position. All the other European judges upheld Nicaragua's case against the United States.[9]

European and Canadian aid to Nicaragua has obstructed not only the U.S. attempt to strangle the country economically, but also its propagandist effort to maintain that Nicaragua is a Soviet dependency. As the North American Congress on Latin America (NACLA) has pointed out, Western aid challenges the U.S. position by suggesting that "Nicaragua could indeed pursue a non-aligned course outside the Soviet bloc".[10] The Reagan administration has therefore tried to use its considerable influence with its European allies to further isolate Nicaragua, as it did with the multilateral banks, Venezuela and Mexico.

The U.S. State Department has generally used diplomatic channels in an attempt to bring European governments 'into line' on Central American issues. In 1981, intense diplomatic pressure from Washington led one European diplomat to comment, "It's a very, very delicate issue right now'', with governments having to ''walk a thin line between their commitment to social justice and their desire for a working relationship with the United States''.[11] Details of such pressure do not usually come to public attention, but several instances have been prominent:

○ Attempting to promote an alternative policy for Central America, the socialist government of Francois Mitterand in France agreed to sell Nicaragua $15.8 million in military equipment. Outrage in Washington, and a meeting with President Reagan in March 1982, caused Mitterand to announce that the armaments remaining to be disbursed (including two Alouette-3 helicopters) ''would face indefinite delays''.[12]

○ When EEC and Central American foreign ministers met in Costa Rica in 1984, it was with the intention of increasing political dialogue and economic cooperation between the two regions. Before the meeting, U.S. Secretary of State George Schultz sent a letter to each of the delegates strongly urging that the initiative ''does not lead to increased economic aid or support for the Sandinistas''.[13] The ministers responded that they had no intention of excluding Nicaragua from a regional agreement. France's Foreign Minister, Claude Cheysson, said further, ''Where does Mr. Reagan come in here? As far as I know, he is not a member of the European Community. As far as I know, he does not belong to a Central American country, and he definitely has nothing to do with Contadora''.

○ In 1986, the Swiss Ministry of Development Cooperation (DEH) received an unusual amount of attention from U.S. State Department representatives concerning Swiss projects in Nicaragua. On one occasion, officials at the Ministry were presented with satellite photos of Swiss projects intended to demonstrate that the projects were 'militarized'. The Ministry, however, was already aware that the rural projects were being guarded by local farmers and protected by trenches because they are often the targets of Contra attacks. On another occasion, a newly-appointed U.S. consul-general in Zurich showed DEH officials slides of a Swiss project in Nicaragua that he had visited shortly before taking up his post. He had presented himself as a tourist, and had spoken only to the local people on the project, not to the DEH representatives. Ministry officials were reported to have remarked that such unusual actions on the part of a U.S. diplomat were ''on the verge of spying''.[14]

○ Major Swiss newspapers, radio and television were also frequently visited by U.S. diplomats, and reportedly received an 'extraordinary' amount of U.S. government documents on Central America and Nicaragua.[15]

○ In Norway, similarly, governmental and non-governmental aid agencies have received extraordinary attention from U.S. Embassy delegates, giving their stance on Central America and expressing disapproval of Norwegian projects in Nicaragua.[16]

○ When President Reagan announced the U.S. trade embargo on Nicaragua and requested allied cooperation during a visit to Europe in May 1985, he was unanimously rebuffed.[17] European governments spoke out against such a drastic measure and offered Nicaragua access to their own markets to overcome the loss of those in the United States. A report of the Institute for Policy Studies summarizes this response in Western Europe and Canada:

> ''Bananas, Nicaragua's largest export affected by the embargo, immediately found markets in Belgium, France, the Netherlands, Ireland and West Germany. France announced its intention to broaden commercial ties with Nicaragua despite the embargo. Italy reaffirmed its commitment to help the Nicaraguans complete a multi-million dollar thermo-electric project. Canadian officials agreed in early June to contribute $7 million to the same project, and have assured Managua that U.S. subsidiaries in Canada would not be affected by the U.S. embargo. Sweden communicated that it was prepared to help Nicaragua overcome the effects of the embargo, and announced plans to increase wheat shipments, aid, and export credits to Managua. The Austrian government approved a $3.5 million credit as 'an Austrian answer to the U.S. embargo against Nicaragua', and declared that Austria would 'not permit anyone to dictate to us how to develop our relations with other small countries'''.[18]

BILATERAL ASSISTANCE FROM INDIVIDUAL EUROPEAN COUNTRIES

Britain, together with the United States, was alone among major aid donors to give more aid to the Somoza dictatorship in its last seven years than to the post-revolutionary government in the seven years since the revolution.[19] British aid since the revolution has been virtually nil, limiting itself essentially to partial funding of British NGO programmes and a few grants to Nicaraguan NGOs.

In general, disbursements of Western European bilateral assistance have remained fairly stable throughout the post-revolutionary period, at around $70 million per year, and increasing to $100 million in 1986 (see Table 14). The stability of such assistance to Nicaragua, however, is being increasingly threatened, not only by pressure from the United States, but also by the rise of conservative governments in Europe and increasing constraints on their budgets. The Netherlands, after making a $130-million five-year commitment for Nicaraguan reconstruction under a Social Democrat-Christian Democrat coalition government, did not renew the programme under the more conservative coalition government that followed. A West German commitment of DM160 million, made by the Social Democratic government of Helmut Schmidt (1979-82) was frozen when a Christian Democrat-dominated coalition came to power in 1982. In France, the Socialist administration elected in 1983 was more generous with Nicaraguan aid than either its predecessor or successor.

The flow of aid has been less erratic from Sweden, which emerged as one of the biggest West European donors after 1979 and in recent years has increased its aid substantially. Finnish aid has also been increasing steadily since 1983. Norway is now opening up official channels of development assistance to Nicaragua. Spain, France and Yugoslavia increased their credits to Nicaragua for imports and repair of equipment in 1985, enabling them to take advantage of trade opportunities created in part by the U.S. trade embargo.

Nevertheless, arguments against aid to Nicaragua echoing the U.S. line on human rights violations and Soviet expansion, are increasingly heard in Europe. The present Dutch government has decided to divide the aid that once went solely to Nicaragua among the five countries of the region, citing the need to support the 'young democracies' in El Salvador, Guatemala, and Honduras.[20] In 1987, France also announced that it will redirect its aid programmes in Central America towards those democratic countries which respect human rights—suggesting that Nicaragua does not fit the bill.[21]

There has been a distinct tendency, however, to use different criteria when measuring the state of human rights in Nicaragua and other countries of Central America. In Nicaragua's war against the Contras there have undeniably been human rights abuses.[22] Yet the restriction of freedom of speech and suspension of *habeas corpus* when a country is at war—as in Nicaragua—cannot be likened to the human rights abuses of the military and by death squads in El Salvador and Guatemala. The Nicaraguan government has publicly denounced cases of human rights violations by military officers, several of which have been brought to trial, found guilty, and punished with prison sentences.[23] In El Salvador and Guatemala, systematic repression, murder, 'disappearances' and torture have been well-documented. At a reported average of nine violent killings per week in Guatemala[24] and over three a day in El Salvador,[25] the offenders are rarely prosecuted.

The decision of some European governments to increase development assistance to the other countries in Central America, if this is done at the expense of programmes in Nicaragua, is unfortunate. There are many impediments to development in El Salvador, Honduras and Guatemala which are comparatively absent in Nicaragua: massive capital flight, government corruption and the absence of a serious agrarian reform programme are some examples.[26]

THE EUROPEAN COMMUNITY

In contrast to the variability of bilateral aid from certain European countries, assistance from the EEC has been remarkably constant, probably as a result of the Community's relative autonomy, its more general perception of European interests, and its role in counterbalancing extreme positions between member states. For example,

> "Within the EEC, the British government has voiced strong political objections to increasing aid to Nicaragua. Answering a parliamentary question in November 1982, a government spokesman said: 'In considering who should benefit we have to take account of the low priority which the government of Nicaragua appears to give to using local resources for social and economic development, as well as their curbs on civil rights, the treatment of minorities, and the continuing military build-up in Nicaragua'. That month, the EEC Foreign Affairs Council decided against allocating a proposed special aid package to Nicaragua. But France and other member States argued successfully for additional funds without discrimination against Nicaragua."[27]

The EEC has distanced itself from U.S. policy in Central America and has actively promoted an alternative approach. Whereas U.S. regional development initiatives like the Caribbean Basin Initiative exclude countries such as Nicaragua and Cuba, the EEC has sought to promote economic and social development in Central America on the basis of regional integration, which includes all the nations in the area. Moreover, the EEC has actually favoured Nicaragua, which received half the total official development assistance allocated to all five Central American countries between 1981 and 1984 (see Table 15).

A breakdown of EEC aid to Nicaragua (see Table 12) shows that 60 percent of total aid consisted of donations of food, reflecting the

Community's chronic problem of disposing of burdensome agricultural surpluses.

ADAPTING AID TO CHANGING PRIORITIES

Most bilateral aid and EEC non-food aid has conventionally been directed toward relatively large-scale development projects, and in fields preferred by donors (see Appendix IV). These preferences have affected donor-readiness to adapt to Nicaragua's changing priorities. Canadian aid, for example, has concentrated on the provision of material and technical assistance to energy development (geothermal generation of electricity and the use of charcoal instead of oil to produce cement), food security (grain storage and milk production), and drinking-water projects. Swedish assistance was allocated primarily to mining, forestry and health service programmes until 1985. Assistance from the Netherlands has been directed to health services, the port sector, and rural development. Concessionary loans from Italy have been earmarked almost entirely for geothermal energy development. Swiss official development assistance was allocated for integrated rural development, drinking-water projects, and school construction. EEC aid consists primarily of food aid, and technical and financial assistance for agriculture and rural development. Norwegian aid, until recently channelled through NGOs and multilateral agencies rather than through bilateral channels, has been given for fertilizer, paper, medicines and medical equipment.

Some countries have shown flexibility, however, in adapting aid from medium- and long-term investments to current expenditure on inputs, spare parts and consumer goods, as Nicaraguan priorities have shifted. The combined effect of defence expenditure and high rates of investment has produced rapid inflation and a fall in living standards for some sectors of the population. Recognizing that this was inevitable, Sweden, Spain and France began providing aid for goods that would keep the Nicaraguan economy afloat. The substantial increase in the Swedish contribution (from approximately $13 million to $23 million between 1985 and 1987) for example, is accounted for primarily by additional agricultural inputs, spare parts for small industry and basic consumer goods destined for peasant families. Different donors have taken different approaches, according to their development assistance policies. Whereas Swedish assistance has remained highly concessionary, Spain and France have responded to Nicaragua's changing priorities by giving credits at more commercial rates.

NON-GOVERNMENTAL AID

Aid to Nicaragua from NGOs and solidarity groups based in Western Europe, Canada and the United States has been impossible to record, but it is probably around $30-50 million per year, of which over 80 percent may be from Western Europe and Canada. An estimated 2,500 Nicaraguan solidarity committees operate all over the world. Over 50 NGOs have permanent representatives in Nicaragua, and many more send aid in various ways.

Although FACS is attempting to coordinate NGO activities and indicate priorities, in practice it only coordinates a small percentage of total NGO aid. There are hundreds of small solidarity projects sponsored by European cities, trade unions, and church groups that are not centrally registered. It was not until 1986 that the Ministry of External Cooperation and some of the regional governments established offices to deal specifically with NGO aid.

While bilateral aid to Nicaragua from some European countries is declining, there are indications that NGO aid may possibly be on the increase. Part of the reason may be that giving aid through NGOs rather than through an official bilateral programme allows donor governments to avoid taking a position and to distance themselves politically from the recipient country. Though the amount of money disbursed by NGOs is considerably smaller than most bilateral aid, it plays a crucial role in that country's development and survival.

In many cases, NGOs have continued to fund projects in Nicaragua when their governments have withdrawn or reduced support. As the Reagan administration heightened the pressure on the Nicaraguan government and economy, some NGOs gave even more aid, despite difficult operating conditions. The amount of NGO aid channelled through FACS, for example, nearly doubled in 1986, from $2.3 to $4.1 million (although part of this increase is accounted for by donations in kind not valued in previous years).

NGO aid mitigates some of the potentially negative features of government aid, such as its bias towards large-scale development projects, and its susceptibility to restrictions on public expenditure. These factors have limited official bilateral and multilateral assistance for small-scale projects and social programmes, and have often been obstacles to assistance that could have counteracted a deterioriation in living standards for some of the population.

NGO aid can have a particularly positive role in urban neighbourhoods, rural communities or cooperatives, since its objectives are usually oriented towards peasant agriculture or small-scale industry, local housing, or basic services such health, education and drinking water. Such aid also plays an important role in strengthening the capacity of the urban and rural poor to organize more effectively and participate in decision-making, through its emphasis on training and its direct support of mass organizations, such as the women's association (AMNLAE), the main trade union organizations (CST and ATC), the farmers' association (UNAG); and the neighbourhood committees (CDS) (see Appendix V). In this way it can contribute to more pluralistic development.

NGOs usually give priority to small-scale participatory projects. Their costs are low compared with those of official aid agencies. They depend on relatively low-paid but highly motivated staff, and often on volunteers who require only that their travel and other expenses be met. Their need for office space is generally minimal, as are their other fixed costs within the country, and all or most of their home-country overhead costs are covered by voluntary contributions.

In addition to helping to prepare and give financial support to small- and medium-scale people-oriented projects of all kinds, NGOs can play an important part in technical assistance and policy formation. They can attract highly capable, well-trained and experienced people (especially young people) in particular fields such as health, education, small industries, small-farming, and cooperatives, who want to help development in Nicaragua. For example, several NGOs have provided first-class mechanics to teach cooperatives to maintain and repair machinery. The Swedish Cooperative Centre has brought volunteers to work with UNAG's farmer cooperative project: the volunteers not only have a great deal of experience with cooperative organization, administration and accounting, but are also professional agriculturists and experienced farmers. Moreover, NGO support of small participatory projects strengthens the capacity and importance of many of their Nicaraguan counterpart organizations. NGO workers in Nicaragua have furthermore facilitated the transfer of local technology by providing professional and personal contacts in their home countries, obtaining additional information when required and sometimes even additional finance.

In the first years after the revolution, many NGOs supported national programmes, such as the Food for Work Campaign, the National Literacy Crusade, the Adult Education Programme and the Popular Health

Campaigns. More recently, NGO attention has shifted, largely to local projects associated with regional or municipal authorities. Many NGOs are also linked to religious organizations which have contributed significant amounts of humanitarian aid as the war and the economic crisis have intensified. For instance, one agency alone in Nicaragua, the Evangelical Committee for Help to Development (CEPAD), serves as a recipient and channel for more than $2 million annually from religious organizations in Western Europe and North America.

The solidarity committees have also been very active in channelling various forms of aid to Nicaragua. A national initiative, the 'Nicaragua Must Survive' campaign, was launched in June 1985, with the support of solidarity organizations throughout the world. It aims to acquire significant quantities of medicines, tools and basic goods, particularly for the rural population. The Canadian organization Tools for Peace, for example, raised more than Canadian $2 million in 1986 to ship medical and technical equipment to Nicaragua.[28] In Europe, five trans-Atlantic cargo ships—which would otherwise have returned virtually empty to Nicaraguan ports—were used in the campaign.

The committees have often helped establish 'twin-city' relationships between city council or local organizations in North America and Western Europe, and cities in Nicaragua. Around 100 cities in Western Europe alone have been helping with cultural exchanges, and supporting projects to improve the physical and social infrastructure of the poorest neighbourhoods in their sister cities. City-linking schemes are a new and innovative factor in the discussion of development cooperation in Western Europe, providing an avenue for the expression of local sympathies for Nicaragua and a channel for those donors who have no infrastructure in Nicaragua for disbursing aid.

A major recipient of NGO aid has been the Nicaraguan Institute for Social Security and Welfare (INSSBI). Another has been the farmers' association (UNAG), which has grown in recent years. The corresponding growth in NGO support to UNAG has reflected not only the increasing strength and organizational capacity of the farmers' association, but also an increasing emphasis on small-scale agriculture and cooperative development—which is partly a result of UNAG's influence on the government. Some NGOs have also preferred to support UNAG rather than the mass organizations more closely connected to the FSLN, following criticism in their home countries.

A 1984 report on NGO aid to Nicaragua[29] and our own analysis of aid channelled through FACS show that the main sources of NGO aid outside the United States are in West Germany (through agencies such as Terre des Hommes, Information Bureau Nicaragua, and Pan para el Mundo) and Canada (through CARE, Cansave, Oxfam and CUSO). The next largest sources are in the Netherlands (NOVIB, Cebemo, Hivos and ICCO), and Belgium (Oxfam). Other significant NGO contributions come from France, Norway, Sweden, Switzerland, and the United Kingdom.

Western European and Canadian governments generally recognize the positive contribution of NGOs, and finance a significant proportion of the aid administered by their NGOs. EEC support for NGO projects in Nicaragua covers up to 50 percent of project costs. Table 16 shows how the EEC contribution to NGO projects in Nicaragua increased from 0.7 million ECUs in 1983 to 2.6 million in 1986 (or approximately the equivalent in dollars). The number of new projects supported each year rose from 19 to 39 in those four years. EEC co-financing of NGO projects in Nicaragua totals nearly ten times that provided to any other Central American country,[30] reflecting an NGO preference for working in Nicaragua.

The significance of NGO aid is particularly apparent in the rural regions of Nicaragua. In Matagalpa in the centre of the country, a small government office, which was established in 1985 to deal with international cooperation, is attempting to help NGOs and other donors make contact with their local counterparts and set priorities in line with government objectives. Although only a partial inventory of NGO projects exists (since NGOs have not been legally obliged to report their activities), the office estimates that there are some 600-700 NGO projects in Matagalpa alone.

These are mostly small projects, with budgets of under $6,000, but there are also several larger ones, some over $100,000 in magnitude. The Dutch aid mission alone has 25 small projects in Matagalpa and the Dutch organization NOVIB has 90, assisting community drinking-water supply, schools, vegetable gardens, housing for displaced persons, health clinics, and agricultural cooperatives. The sum of this aid amounts to several million dollars annually in Matagalpa alone, excluding maintenance costs. Although Matagalpa is one of the most favoured areas for Western European aid, it is only one of 16 departments in the country, indicating that the total amount of this kind of aid may be very large indeed.

At any one time, there may be as many as 2,000 people from NGOs working in the country: some of the organizations have 20-40 technicians in Nicaragua, and they generally operate for at least a few months. Precise data on the number of volunteers do not exist, however. When the Nicaraguan government decided to withdraw foreigners from the war zones in August 1986, authorities were surprised by the numbers who came to a regional meeting called in Estelí. Whereas only a few dozen NGO volunteers or 'cooperantes' were registered, an estimated 700 turned up. Another 300 appeared for a similar meeting in Matagalpa. These numbers do not include the hundreds of 'brigadistas' who arrive from all over the world at the end of each year to pick coffee.

There has been criticism of some NGOs operating in Nicaragua. A number of NGOs with relatively large aid programmes there have no permanent representatives in the country, which impedes both the effective monitoring and evaluation of project implementation, and the initiation of feasibility studies for new projects. Second, several projects supported by NGOs are small, isolated and disconnected from regional and national development plans. Third, there is still a tendency among some NGOs to compete rather than cooperate—although this has diminished greatly—and to follow their own preferences more than the changing needs in Nicaragua.

The NGO presence in Nicaragua has done more than simply promote community organization and participation in development. NGOs have put Nicaraguan groups in direct contact with support groups in their home countries, which are willing to provide additional assistance. Furthermore, the NGOs' home offices usually have informal—and sometimes official—contacts with their governments' aid agencies and with political leaders, to whom they present a more informed picture of Nicaragua. They also disseminate information about Nicaragua to the general public in Western Europe and North America. NGO personnel, volunteers and participants in solidarity tours return and speak to other interested groups about their experiences. Their news generally contradicts U.S. propaganda about a totalitarian, anti-popular government. Many have also witnessed at first-hand the aftermath of Contra atrocities and the terror these spread among the rural population.

Chapter IV examines the role of foreign aid in the implementation of projects in Nicaragua, in five specific projects, as an illustration of how development assistance policies are being practically realized.

Notes to Chapter 3

1. W. Grabendorff, "La Crisis Centro Americana: ¿ Europa Occidental vs. Estados Unidos?", *Cuadernos Semestrales*, no.12, CIDE, Mexico, 1982, p. 296, (authors' translation).

2. Quoted in C. Brundenius and V. Bye, "Towards Broader Economic Relations between the State and the Nordic Countries and the Caribbean Basin," *PRIO Report 20/86*, Oslo, 1986, p. 45.

3. Quoted in CAIS, *Nicaragua Briefing*, July 1986.

4. M.O. Colin, op.cit., p.11.

5. C. Brundenius and V. Bye, op.cit., p. 44.

6. See Chavez, M., "La Política Exterior de Nicaragua Respecto a Europa Occidental 1979—1985: Avance de Investigación," INIES, mimeo, Managua, 1986.

7. Foreign Office Memo from James W. Watt, October 1984; letter from J. M. M. Vereker to Hugh Arbuthnott, February 1985; see also *The Observer*, 26 May, 1985.

8. Nicaragua Solidarity Campaign, "The British Connection," *Nicaragua Special Report*, London, 1987, p. 1.

9. Ibid., p. 1.

10. R. Matthews, "The Limits of Friendship: Nicaragua and the West", *NACLA: Report on the Americas*, May/June, 1985, New York, p. 29.

11. *The New York Times*, 30 July, 1981; quoted in R. Matthews, op.cit., p. 28.

12. *The Washington Post*, 10 July, 1982; quoted in R. Matthews, op.cit., p. 30.

13. *International Herald Tribune*, 1 October, 1984.

14. R. Berger, "American Pressure on Switzerland: Switzerland Urged to Withdraw Aid from Nicaragua", *Tages Anzeige*, September 11, 1986, (authors' translation), see also A. Lietti, "Pressions Americaines sur la Suisse," *L'Hebdo*, 18 September, 1986, pp. 22-23.

15. Ibid.

16. Interviews with several Norwegian authorities and organizations dealing with development assistance, Oslo, Norway, May 1987.

17. *International Herald Tribune*, 6 and 9 May, 1985.

18. D. Siegel and T. Spaulding, *Outcast Among Allies: The International Costs of Reagan's War Against Nicaragua*, Institute for Policy Studies, Washington D.C., 1985, p. 14.

19. Nicaragua Solidarity Campaign, op.cit., p. 5.

20. "Regiobeleid Midden Amerika en de Andes-landen", Tweede Kamer Notitie 20014, no. 2; and *de Volkskrant*, 10 August, 1987.

21. See *Le Monde*, 13 January, 1987; *Le Figaro*, 9 February, 1987.

22. See Washington Office on Latin America report, "Nicaragua: Violations of the Laws of War by Both Sides", February-December 1985 and "Nicaragua:

Violations of the Laws of War by Both Sides, First Supplement'', January-March 1986.
23. See *ENVIO*, ''Derechos Humanos: El Expediente de Nicaragua'', Instituto Histórico Centroamericano, no. 76, October 1987, p. 26.
24. Americas Watch and British Parliamentary Human Rights Group, *Human Rights in Guatemala During President Cerezo's First Year*, New York, 1987, pp. 7, 30-31. Over 100 violent killings per month were reported in the Guatemalan press in 1986. Guatemalan journalists following the matter told Americas Watch that 80 percent of the cases reported in the press in the first half of 1986 had some characteristics of executions and 'disappearances' by the security forces or paramilitary groups. Assessing whether political repression is the motivation behind deaths and disappearances is very difficult in Guatemala. Americas Watch reports that the editors of *Central America Report* (based in Guatemala City) counted 224 politically related killings and at least 110 politically related disappearances from January 1986 to November 15 of that year. This is an average of nine cases per week.
25. Instituto de Derechos Humanos, *Los Derechos Humanos en El Salvador en 1986*, Universidad Centroamericana ''José Simeón Cañas'', San Salvador, 1987, p. 20. The figure includes 1,104 deaths attributed to the armed forces and 118 deaths attributed to right-wing death squads.
26. See fuller discussion in S. Barraclough and M. Scott, *The Rich Have Already Eaten*, Transnational Institute, Amsterdam, 1987.
27. D. Melrose, *Nicaragua: The Threat of A Good Example?*, Oxfam Public Affairs Unit, Oxford, U.K., 1985, p. 49.
28. Canadian-Caribbean-Central American Policy Alternatives (CAPA), Information Circular, August 1987.
29. F. Tomic and M.O. Colin, ''Relación FIR-ONG, 1979-84'', mimeo, Managua, 1984.
30. A. Reithinger, ''Partners in Development: the EEC, the NGOs, and the Peoples of the Third World'', *The Courier*, July/August 1987, p. 73.

TABLE 12

EUROPEAN ECONOMIC COMMUNITY AID TO NICARAGUA, 1979-85

(thousands of ECU)

Type of aid	1979	1980	1981	1982	1983	1984	1985
Food aid	4,060	6,250	9,700	8,310	9,810	9,110	15,526
Technical and financial aid	2,500	2,960	8,250	10,400	3,500	—	2,500
Other*	662	938	1,332	1,089	1,851	1,670	2,852
Total	**7,222**	**10,148**	**19,282**	**19,799**	**15,161**	**10,780**	**20,878**

* Includes aid channelled through NGOs, emergency aid, aid for refugees and displaced persons, technical assistance, studies and training.

Source: EEC.

TABLE 13

NICARAGUAN TRADE WITH WESTERN EUROPE AND CANADA, 1977-86

(millions of US dollars)

Year	EXPORTS			IMPORTS			TRADE BALANCE		
	EEC*	Others**	Total	EEC*	Others**	Total	EEC*	Others**	Total
1977	181	12	193	96	53	149	85	-41	44
1978	180	10	190	68	37	105	112	-27	85
1979	149	14	163	35	17	52	114	- 3	111
1980	130	45	175	70	35	105	60	10	70
1981	106	52	158	115	54	169	- 9	- 2	-11
1982	94	39	133	109	45	154	-15	- 6	-21
1983	111	17	128	78	58	136	33	-41	- 8
1984	113	38	151	103	85	188	10	-47	-37
1985	118	34	152	109	89	198	9	-55	-46
1986 +	117	5	123	148	62	210	-31	-57	-88

* West Germany, Belgium, Denmark, France, Ireland, Italy, Netherlands, United Kingdom, Greece. In 1986, includes Spain and Portugal.

** Austria, Norway, Sweden, Switzerland, Spain, Portugal, Canada. In 1986, excludes Spain and Portugal.

\+ Preliminary figures.

Source: Ministry of External Trade.

TABLE 14

DISBURSEMENTS OF OFFICIAL DEVELOPMENT ASSISTANCE FROM WESTERN EUROPE* AND CANADA TO NICARAGUA, 1981-86

(millions of US dollars)

Country	1981	1982	1983	1984	1985	1986**
Austria	0.7	8.7	8.1	0.5	4.4	1.3
Belgium	0.8	0.6	0.5	0.5	0.5	0.7
Canada	5.6	2.3	6.2	8.8	5.8	4.3
Denmark	1.4	0.3	1.6	0.8	0.9	3.2
Finland	—	2.5	1.6	3.0	3.2	7.1
France	1.4	8.5	8.7	8.5	7.0	14.1
Germany	12.0	8.5	6.9	4.5	4.7	8.0
Italy	5.0	2.5	3.2	2.3	4.3	13.7
Netherlands	15.8	23.9	17.6	21.2	15.7	19.2
Norway	0.4	2.1	2.3	5.7	5.0	11.5
Sweden	3.9	9.3	10.6	13.7	12.6	17.5
Switzerland	0.8	1.4	2.5	2.1	2.9	3.6
United Kingdom	0.1	0.1	0.1	—	0.2	0.1
Total	**47.9**	**70.7**	**69.9**	**71.6**	**67.2**	**104.3**

* Excluding Spain.

** Provisional figures.

Source: OECD, see *Geographical Distribution of Financial Flows to Developing Countries*, 1981/1984, and 1982/1985.

TABLE 15

EEC MULTILATERAL AND BILATERAL OFFICIAL DEVELOPMENT ASSISTANCE TO CENTRAL AMERICA* 1981-84

(millions of US dollars)

Country	**1981**	**1982**	**1983**	**1984**
Nicaragua	46.7	51.6	44.6	52.8
Costa Rica	19.4	14.1	11.5	15.9
El Salvador	3.4	3.6	6.5	5.6
Guatemala	8.3	7.4	7.3	6.4
Honduras	15.3	22.4	20.0	27.7
Central America	**93.1**	**99.1**	**89.9**	**108.4**

* Excluding Ireland and Greece.

Source: OECD.

TABLE 16

EEC CONTRIBUTIONS TO EUROPEAN NGOS FOR PROJECTS IN NICARAGUA 1983-86

	1983	**1984**	**1985**	**1986**
Number of new projects supported	19	20	29	39
EEC contribution (mn ECU)*	0.7	1.4	1.2	2.6
Total cost of projects (mn ECU)*	1.9	3.4	3.7	7.2

* 1 ECU = \$1.00 (August 1986).

Source: EEC.

4 AN ASSESSMENT OF PROJECT IMPLEMENTATION IN NICARAGUA

This chapter looks at the actual implementation of projects, the problems encountered, and the response of donor agencies. Five specific projects supported mainly with bilateral assistance and NGO funds are examined, based on project evaluations, visits to project sites, and interviews with representatives of European and Canadian development agencies, NGOs, project directors, technicians, and their Nicaraguan counterparts.

The criteria used in assessing the effectiveness of an aid project pose problems. It must first be said that the effectiveness of aid depends as much on the objectives and priorities of the development strategy, as on the technical efficacy in the use of external assistance. For example, it can be said that aid to the Somoza regime was effective in contributing to the rapid growth of Nicaragua's agro-exports and GDP during the 1960s and early 1970s. Aid helped to consolidate a repressive agro-export development model, highly dependent on markets and financing associated with mostly U.S.-based transnational corporations. Despite considerable corruption, aid helped create infrastructure and other favourable conditions for private investment, both foreign and domestic. Capital flight was not a major problem until the development model began to deteriorate in the mid-1970s, when demand for Nicaraguan exports in world markets slackened, and internal unrest grew. The aid was never effective, however, in improving social conditions, promoting human rights, greater political democracy and popular participation, or in constructing a more diversified and integrated economy—which were not among the government's development objectives at the time.

To assess the role of aid in the post-revolutionary period, we have therefore used general criteria: the contribution towards people's livelihoods; access to basic goods and services; increase in popular participation by low-income groups; and steps towards the achievement of a more autonomous and diversified economy. This means linking agriculture and industry, and increasing both net foreign exchange earnings, and the country's capacity to mobilize domestic resources to meet its development goals and compete in world markets. This depends on world market conditions and on the terms under which aid is granted, as well as on how well the aid is used in implementing projects, how well the projects are conceived in relation to the country's development strategy, and how viable that strategy is in itself.

Opinions of Donor Agency Representatives

Present project experience contrasts sharply with that before the revolution. Oxfam, one of the oldest NGOs working in Nicaragua, describes some of the difficulties encountered in its own assistance programme during the Somoza period, in a recent report:

> "The Managua earthquake [of 1972, which killed up to 20,000 people] was to provide new insights into poverty and corruption under Somoza. ... A National Emergency Committee, set up under President Somoza's control and run by the National Guard, institutionalized the misappropriation of emergency relief. Realizing that relief supplies were being syphoned off and sold by the National Guard, Oxfam's Field Director talked Mrs. Somoza into giving permission to bypass the official distribution system. This meant waiting in the air traffic control tower for the right plane to be spotted, then careering onto the tarmac to get the trucks loaded before the National Guard arrived on the scene."[1]

Referring to the dramatically changed environment for project execution following the revolution, the Oxfam report further states:

> "during the Somoza years, ...doubts [were raised] about whether to attempt to work in Nicaragua at all. Subsequently, since 1979, the scope for development has been enormous, with remarkable progress achieved in health, literacy and a more equitable distribution of resources."[2]

Discussions with directors and representatives of other agencies in Nicaragua confirmed Oxfam's view that development organizations can work more productively in present-day war-torn Nicaragua than they could under Somoza, or, for that matter, in many other Third World countries.

Aid agencies and lending institutions alike have generally rated Nicaragua's development record highly. A 1983 publication of the World Council of Churches commented:

> "What we see is a government faced with tremendous problems, some seemingly insuperable, bent on a great experiment which, though precarious and incomplete at many points, provides hope to the poor sectors of society, improves the conditions of education, literacy, and health, and for the first time offers the Nicaraguan people a modicum of justice for all, rather than a society offering privilege exclusively to the wealthy ...and to the powerful."[3]

Similarly, in our interviews, the director of a major European bilateral programme saw the government's development efforts as directed toward the "betterment of the general public rather than a small elitist group."[4] The Inter-American Development Bank likewise concluded in 1983 that, "Nicaragua has made noteworthy progress in the social sector, which is laying a solid foundation for long-term socio-economic development."[5]

For many development agencies, the important difference in Nicaragua today is that there is a considerable degree of coherence between their own development policy and that of the Nicaraguan government. For both, the task of development includes meeting the basic needs of the poor majority of the population—in health, education, housing, and food production. The substantial quantity of NGO aid to Nicaragua is generally attributable to this compatibility between NGO goals and those of the government. Indeed, the two are so compatible that, in addition to many small-scale projects, several NGOs have begun supporting much larger and more official projects in Nicaragua than those they fund in most other parts of the world. Nicaragua is the only Latin American country to have priority status in the Swedish aid programme because, as one Swedish aid agency representative put it, "The aims of the Nicaraguan government development policy coincide exactly with the principles upon which our policy is based."[6]

The increasing amounts of Swedish bilateral aid to Nicaragua reflect not only strong political links between the two governments, but also the Swedish government's recognition that aid in Nicaragua has been put to good use. The bottlenecks and delays in many African and Asian countries where Swedish aid is concentrated have not been present on anything like the same scale in Nicaragua. There has been a steady increase in Swedish aid: from SEK 46 million in 1982/3, to 125 million in 1986. The total was expected to reach 160 million in 1987 (or approximately $23 million).

Many representatives of development organizations shared this view. The serious development objectives of the Nicaraguan government and its willingness to cooperate have made the country particularly attractive to development and relief agencies. The advantages of government involvement in development projects and programmes have considerably outweighed the disadvantages, even for agencies like Oxfam, who have in the past worked mainly with grass-roots organizations. With few exceptions, the agency and project directors interviewed said they were content with their relationship with the government. Where there were criticisms, there was also an acknowledgement that "the Nicaraguan government has been open and helpful and very willing to facilitate the execution of projects''.[7]

In some of the other Central American countries, the absence of cooperation and openness on the part of governments has meant that in many cases the NGOs are unwilling to work with them. One European aid agency representative compared his experience in Nicaragua with that in other countries in the region, saying, ''In Nicaragua you can work with the government; we wouldn't touch the governments of most of the other Central American countries.''[8]

Representatives of almost all the agencies agreed that there were other serious obstacles to their development efforts in most other Central American countries, which did not exist in Nicaragua. It was pointed out that the human rights situation in other countries in the region differed drastically from that in Nicaragua: ''In several other Central American countries, people get killed for doing this kind of work.''[9] Another representative noted that much of the aid going to other countries, particularly El Salvador, was absorbed in simply coping with the effects of the war through refugee programmes, whereas in Nicaragua, an agency can contribute to actual development. Those interviewed also testified to the prevalence of corruption and misuse of funds by most other governments in the region, and the relative absence of such practices in Nicaragua.

In Nicaragua, of course, there have been cases of serious misuse of aid. Examples we encountered included:

- Material aid earmarked for one project, at one point, being syphoned off by FACS to another activity without the donor agency's prior approval.
- One donor to a relief agency withdrawing a quarter of a million dollars of support, following excessive delays by the government's Planning and Budget Office in approving a project.
- An agency without permanent representation in Nicaragua visiting one community to inspect the final stages of its project with the UNAG, and finding that the community had never even heard of the project.

More generally, present conditions in Nicaragua have not made the work of development organizations easy. With the desperate economic situation and the U.S. trade embargo have come soaring inflation, a lack of transport, spare parts, office supplies, and other equipment. These have made project implementation difficult, and budget estimations nearly impossible. Several agency representatives also felt the Nicaraguan government had given insufficient priority to the repair and maintenance of machinery and equipment brought into the country.

Project directors in Managua were very disturbed by the way skilled or recently trained personnel can leave a project, wasting project resources and causing enormous difficulties in fulfilling objectives. Personnel have gone over to the informal and private sectors where earnings are much higher. The need to defend the country has also absorbed not only scarce financial and economic resources, but also much of the nation's human resources, and project participants are conscripted regularly. Emigration has further exacerbated the problem, particularly among technical and professional staff. A number of agency representatives considered that the lack of middle- and higher-level management could pose a serious threat to future operations.

The war itself is, of course, a major concern for development agencies, and affects project and programme execution, not only indirectly by absorbing valuable economic and human resources, but also directly through attacks on cooperatives, grain storage facilities, health centres, schools, day-care centres, and houses. The Contra war has been economically and psychologically damaging, for those who survive Contra attacks. They may spend months or years working (often without pay in their spare time) to build a school, clinic, house or cooperative, then find it reduced to rubble in a day.

More recently, the Contras have succeeded in further heightening intimidation within development organizations—by killing technicians sent from the donor countries themselves. In 1983, one French and one German doctor were killed in separate incidents. While there were no Europeans killed in 1984 and 1985, six European technicians died in Contra attacks in 1986—two from Switzerland, and the others from Spain, Belgium, France and West Germany. The head of one bilateral programme said, "Murdering technicians is a new tactic of the Contras and we are very fearful of this."[10] In April 1987, the first U.S. technician was killed—a volunteer working on hydro-electric projects in the northern interior region of the country.

Nicaragua has now been divided into zones of relative security. In July 1986, the government withdrew all foreigners from the war zones, following Contra declarations which threatened the lives of foreigners working in these areas, and the ambush of two civilian pickup trucks by Contra forces in July 1986 which killed five people, including a French-born Nicaraguan, a Swiss, and a West German volunteer. Some donor countries, notably Italy, West Germany, and Switzerland, have imposed their own demarcation limits, restricting project work in much of the northern and interior regions. The Swiss government has stopped co-financing new Swiss projects in these zones. Thus the war has imposed tight limits on development efforts in some rural areas—where they are most needed.

The difficulties of project implementation are due not only to the war and to external destabilization of the economy. Other problems are the result of deficient Nicaraguan management and a large and complex bureaucracy, as summarized below:[11]

- problems and delays in disbursing committed funds;
- difficulties in distributing imported equipment and materials: notably bottlenecks at the port of Corinto and limited internal transport;
- delays in the purchasing process due to Nicaraguan unfamiliarity with procedures when dealing with new suppliers;
- unfamiliarity with the complex mechanisms of bilateral cooperation;
- difficulties in obtaining a favourable position in business dealings with suppliers and financiers.

Many of these problems are due to the inexperience of Nicaraguan technical personnel, who have to deal with increasing volumes of imports and development assistance. Many skilled persons left the country after Somoza's fall, and the country has been plagued by educational underdevelopment—the legacy of the previous regime.

While agency representatives and foreign project personnel often stress the problems that arise from having to rely on largely inexperienced and unskilled Nicaraguans, they also have difficulty in bringing qualified personnel to Nicaragua. Many West European and Canadian aid programmes were previously concentrated in Africa and Asia. For several donor countries, involvement in Nicaragua required extending their work to a new area of the globe, with a different culture and language. The directors of the Swedish and Canadian bilateral assistance attested to the difficulties of finding in their own country, qualified people, with development experience, who could speak Spanish.

Further problems result from the involvement and support of the Nicaraguan government. One drawback has been that large-scale government promotion of projects addressing basic needs gives rise to a potentially paternalistic approach to development. Social programmes and projects imposed 'from above' can be badly executed if the intended beneficiaries do not participate in their design and implementation. One NGO representive, who also had experience of projects in Guatemala, remarked that in societies where the government does not actively support social programmes, community and popular organizations often take a more direct role in project design and implementation, and may use funds more efficiently than sometimes occurs in Nicaragua. In recognition of this problem, in Southern Zelaya on the Atlantic Coast, a Department of Community Promotion has been established to link projects more closely to needs the local communities perceive themselves, and to increase the involvement of the local population.

The channelling of funds primarily through the Ministry of External Cooperation and FACS, in order to plan and regulate the use of external resources—has imposed serious constraints on the limited number of qualified personnel in these institutions and their capacity to cope with the volume of aid entering Nicaragua. FACS, with a technical staff of less than 30 people, for example, has been involved in finding funds and monitoring the implementation of approximately 300 projects between 1982 and 1986, and presently oversees the implementation of 120 projects dispersed throughout the country.

Bilateral agencies, NGOs and solidarity organizations have all been concerned by bureaucratic delays in identifying appropriate projects, disbursing funds and material aid, monitoring project implementation, and accounting for the use of funds. However, many aid agency representatives saw clear improvements in the organizational and administrative capacity of both FACS and government agencies at the national and regional levels, particularly during 1986 and 1987.

The government itself has also publicly voiced concern about the use or misuse of aid. An in-depth report published in July 1986 by the Sandinista newspaper *Barricada*, for example, criticised the role of the state in administering aid: "Many errors have been committed. Incidences of neglect and bureaucratization have cost tens of thousands of dollars which means fewer schools, health clinics, technical training projects, etc."[12] Efficient use of external resources was made a central guideline in the 1987 economic plan.

PROJECTS ILLUSTRATING THE USE OF WESTERN AID

The five projects we assessed were chosen from a wide range of fields—agriculture, basic goods supply, education, health/work safety, and communications. The size and location of the projects varied considerably. Given the limits of this study, the choice of projects was influenced by the existence of prior evaluations and the availability of project personnel for meetings and site visits. These projects are not an exhausive sample, but illustrate the type and range of projects being supported by Western aid. Our examination focused on problems encountered, and progress made in project implementation; but we had neither time nor resources for an in-depth evaluation. We make some reference in our discussion of each project to issues being debated internally about priorities in the use of aid.

The following projects were selected:

- Chiltepe, a large-scale, capital-intensive, dairy and genetic improvement project near the capital, Managua. The project is primarily supported by the Canadian government, the World Food Programme, and a soft loan from the Inter-American Development Bank;
- ECODEPA, a programme organized by the Nicaraguan farmers' association (UNAG) with support from the Swedish government and a number of NGOs, to supply small farmers with vital production inputs and consumer goods;
- 'Schools in the Valleys', an ambitious school construction project supported by SWISSAID and the Swiss government, located in the south-western region of the country;
- A Pesticide Health and Safety Programme, administered by CARE (Nicaragua) and supported by several U.S. and Canadian NGOs. The project aims to reduce poisoning and environmental contamination, caused by excessive use and careless pesticide application, mainly in the cotton-growing northern Pacific region of the country;
- Videonic, a video training and production centre in Managua, supported by several Western European and North American NGOs.

These projects reflect the scope that exists for cooperation according to different conceptions of development, fields of experience, expertise, and budgets. They also highlight the major constraints on the execution of projects in Nicaragua. A discussion of these constraints, and our conclusions, follows the five case studies.

CHILTEPE

The Chiltepe dairy and genetic improvement project near Managua is one of the biggest of the large-scale, technologically sophisticated, development projects in the ambitious investment programme launched by the Sandinista government in the early 1980s. It has been valued at over $25 million, and is the subject of considerable debate about the appropriateness of Sandinista investment strategy. Its critics have said that it could increase Nicaragua's technological dependency, that mechanization could displace labour; that an underdeveloped economy can not have the material, human and administrative resources to service a project of such scale and sophistication; and that the thousands of cattle imported from Canada may not adapt to tropical conditions. Some have also doubted the State's capacity to manage a project of this nature. Now that the construction phase of the project is largely complete and considerable quantities of milk are being produced, the validity of these criticisms can be examined.

The major objectives of the project are the rapid expansion of national milk production, reduction of powdered milk imports, and genetic improvement of the national cattle stock.

International financial and material support for the project has come from five main sources. The principal contributors have been the Canadian government and the Inter-American Development Bank, who loaned $10.4 million and $4.5 million respectively. The World Food Programme contributed large quantities of milk powder, the sale of which provided a considerable share of the local currency costs of the project. East Germany and the Soviet Union have also contributed smaller amounts, totalling one million dollars.

The principal components imported with these funds included approximately 3,000 Holstein calves from Canada, 56 milking equipment units from Sweden, 8 pivot irrigation systems from Spain, and 60 tractors from the Soviet Union.

Before the revolution, only a quarter of the 7,000 arable hectares on the Chiltepe peninsula were used, producing only 4.3 million litres of milk a year, and employing 300 labourers. Although the project will not be fully on-stream until 1992, in 1986 it was already producing 13 million litres, or about 10 percent of national milk output. Moreover, production is increasing rapidly, from 10 million litres in 1985, to an estimated 18 million in 1987. The project presently employs 750 people, the size of the herd has increased to 12,000 head, including 3,500 milking cows. Some 800 hectares are already under irrigation. By 1992/3, the project is expected to produce 35 million litres (30 percent of present national production), using all 7,000 hectares of agricultural land. By then, the herd should have reached nearly 17,000 head, of which 7,000 would be milking cows. Some 1,200 hectares would be under irrigation and the project would employ 1,000 people.

The project has been delayed by a variety of problems. The construction company had insufficient capacity for the project. More generally, the state sector had limited experience in executing projects of this scale. Other factors delaying the project include:

- planning limitations: the original plans did not consider in detail a number of important areas, associated, for example, with training personnel, and the project's feed and energy needs. Regarding the latter, Chiltepe's director remarked, "This project was drawn up believing that there would always be electricity. In actual fact, we have blackouts nearly every day. This causes considerable disruption and increases our costs."

- restrictions and delays in obtaining local finance to cover the project's local currency costs, in part due to inflation.
- delays in obtaining the Inter-American Development Bank loan, due largely to lack of technical documentation to support the loan application.
- insufficient construction materials and machinery. Much of the road-building machinery lies idle for lack of spare parts.
- shortages of technical and professional staff, many of whom have left the project in search of higher wages.
- shortages of unskilled labourers, both because of low salaries and conscription. Also, until recently, the project paid little attention to the provision of social services for the workers.

These problems delayed work on the project by nearly two years. When it began in 1982, the construction phase was scheduled for completion in 1985. In December 1986, 95 percent of the physical components (including 56 farming units each capable of sheltering, feeding and milking 150 cows; irrigation equipment, and 120 kilometres of road) were in place and full completion was expected in early 1987. By the end of 1988 the herd is expected to have reached its full size.

Modification and innovation of the original plans have been essential in bringing the project to its current state. In order to reduce the córdoba costs of the project, for example, the design of the cattle installations was altered: this saved up to 50 percent on construction costs. To overcome the lack of manpower, the project has actively sought to integrate female workers from nearby towns and communities. Now approximately 20 percent of the work force is made up of women. Also, in order to retain workers, more attention is being paid to the provision of social services and food. At the time of writing, a 28-hectare vegetable plot was being prepared to supply the canteen and local communities.

The financial viability of the project is in question, however. On paper, there would seem to be no major problem. Thirty-five million litres of milk (the estimated 1992 production) converted to milk powder at international market prices would save $12 million a year in foreign exchange, and would undoubtedly make the project quite viable financially, with a payback within 8 years and a profit margin of 12 percent.

Serious problems have intervened, however. First, Nicaragua receives most of its powdered milk imports as donations, and these are drawn from large surpluses in donor countries. This raises an obvious question: should not Nicaragua just rely on donations, even though these can be unstable (as was seen in 1981 when the United States cut off credits for wheat imports)? The Nicaraguan government is probably wise not to base its long term plans on the goodwill of Western governments, but rather to channel resources towards increasing self-sufficiency in basic food production.

Second, the state enterprise that runs the Chiltepe project experienced considerable financial difficulties and incurred major losses in 1986. This was due not to inefficient operation, but to the low official price set by the government for milk. Whereas the company was selling each gallon of milk for 430 córdobas, it required 820 córdobas to cover its production costs. This was less than the new official price set at the end of the year, in the course of an investigation into declining milk production. If problems like these can be resolved, Chiltepe should eventually become remunerative.

Third, a capital-intensive project of this nature requires considerable foreign exchange to cover depreciation. Chiltepe does not bring in foreign exchange and must rely on allocations from the government. To cover depreciation, the project needs to import goods valued at approximately $100,000 a year. This is likely to become a major bottleneck, given the severe shortage of foreign exchange and the virtual absence of a local capital-goods industry. It is probably fair to say that the original planners did not give sufficient consideration to problems of technological dependency. As the director of the project explained, it is over-mechanized for an underdeveloped country like Nicaragua. Irrigation tubes, for example, have traditionally been moved by ox-cart, but now there is a total reliance on tractors. The rapid introduction of modern equipment and machinery has also meant rapid depreciation due to handling by inexperienced personnel.

The other major problem likely to affect future production is a shortage of animal feed, of which much is needed in a project of this type and scale. In addition, the project is located in an area of low rainfall, making animal feed harder to produce. Moreover, a sharp fall in cotton production, and therefore in the availability of cotton seed meal, has meant drawing more on other sources of feed. In order to overcome this, the project has acquired 500 hectares of Chiltepe's irrigated land to produce its own feed. While this should resolve Chiltepe's feed problems, it will mean, of course, less grain for other consumers, such as the general population or the poultry industry. The project has plans to build a $1.5 million feed plant, although at a national level there is excess capacity in the animal feed industry, and the government is now seeking to restrict new public investment projects.

Despite the delays and problems, the government and donors agree that project implementation has been a success. On the basis of previous experience with cattle projects in Africa, Canadian experts believed that the mortality rate of calves shipped from Canada could reach 10 percent. In practice, only 2 percent died. Many also believed that the radical change in climate would hinder the development of the herd, so yields would be low. However, against original estimates of 13 litres per cow per day, the first yields have reached 18 litres per cow per day, and are expected to remain high.

Canadian praise for the dedication of the Nicaraguan counterparts in implementing the project, is reciprocated by Nicaragua. Canadian assistance had clear advantages over that provided by the Inter-American Development Bank. First, Canadian disbursements were far more rapid than those of the IDB. Second, the cattle selected carefully by the Canadian government and provincial authorities were of higher quality than those purchased under the international tendering system used by the IDB. Third, the Canadian government continues to demonstrate an interest in the project, while IDB concern ceased once disbursements ended.

The project seems remarkably well organized and efficiently run. Each farming unit is independent from the others, considerably reducing the risk of disease, and can be operated by just three people. The ratio of one person to 50 cows compares favourably with the traditional ratio of one to ten cows—of particular importance in a country where labour scarcity is one of the main constraints on production.

Chiltepe came on-stream at an opportune moment, when national milk production—and particularly the sale of milk to the processing plants—was falling sharply. Now suppliers of pasteurized milk to urban consumers in Managua and other Pacific coastal cities rely on Chiltepe. The project is clearly an important component of the national food system, and appears to be working well.

In the words of the director of the Nicaraguan Food Programme, "When all around us we see production and projects being destroyed and hampered by the war and the economic crisis, it's refreshing to come to Chiltepe and see that we are capable of building something that really works."

Perhaps the fundamental question hanging over the project is whether resources used in Chiltepe would not have been better employed in trying to stimulate production in other sectors. The government now admits that declining or stagnant production levels among peasant and larger commercial farmers stem not only from war conditions and foreign exchange shortages, but also from a planning bias towards concentrating resources in slow-yielding investment projects, and in the state sector. It seems that an attempt is now being made to redress the balance in favour of other sectors. A dairy project even larger than Chiltepe was recently started in the interior, incorporating not only state farms, but also cooperatives and private producers. The government also initiated a comprehensive development strategy for the cattle sector in early 1987—which pays particular attention to the circumstances and interests of medium- and small-scale private producers.

ECODEPA

The ECODEPA programme was started in late 1984 by the National Union of Farmers and Cattlemen (UNAG), which represents the interests of small- and medium-scale farmers. Financial support was received from the government of Sweden, and technical assistance from the Swedish Cooperative Centre (CCS, which is an NGO). ECODEPA began as a small programme in Matagalpa designed to supply small farmers in isolated rural zones affected by the war with vital production inputs and consumer goods.

By 1986, the ECODEPA programme had become one of the more exciting and promising development projects in rural Nicaragua. It was responsible for distributing a variety of vital imported goods through an extensive network of peasant cooperative stores. By the end of that year, it was also distributing domestically produced goods, such as clothing and barbed wire. In addition, many ECODEPA cooperative stores stocked seeds, fertilizers, herbicides and pesticides for use by state agencies in isolated or difficult rural areas. Moreover, some of the cooperative stores were acquiring experience in marketing corn, beans and other produce of small-scale farmers. All this was being done with a high degree of peasant participation and minimal administrative personnel and costs, at better prices for both producers and consumers than those charged by private traders.

Additional NGO support came in 1986 from Oxfam America, Oxfam 'U.K.' and HIVOS in the Netherlands. UNAG estimated that ECODEPA stores had supplied over half Nicaragua's 200,000 small farmers with some production inputs or consumer goods. About 70,000 farmers had purchased 212,000 machetes (a basic Nicaraguan peasant tool) from ECODEPA outlets during 1985 and 1986.

ECODEPA's rapid growth and its success in helping large numbers of small farmers confront basic production and consumption constraints through their own efforts, illustrate how a relatively small amount of European aid can spark off an important, popular-based, development initiative.

In many countries, agrarian reforms and rural development efforts have failed to benefit peasant producers. Private merchants or state agencies have failed to provide them with necessary inputs and consumer goods at prices they can afford, or to purchase their products at prices high enough for them to maintain themselves or increase production.

While this problem is universal, it became particularly acute in post-revolutionary Nicaragua with the U.S. economic blockade and armed attacks by U.S.-backed Contras. Rural-urban trade was seriously disrupted and an estimated 250,000 inhabitants have had to abandon their homes and land. The state agencies set up to supply rural producers and buy their products were short of resources, deeply involved in the war effort; and sometimes inefficient, or unresponsive to the immediate needs of peasant producers. The shortage of foreign exchange made it impossible even to maintain pre-revolutionary import levels, to say nothing of expanding them to meet growing demand. Getting basic supplies to small farmers (especially those in frontier regions) and bringing out their products became one of the most crucial problems facing the survival economy. Its solution was vital for the war effort, the livelihoods of the rural population, and producing and marketing enough food for urban consumers.

ECODEPA, now a national cooperative enterprise, began working towards its own legal charter in late 1986, as UNAG's independent economic branch. It has an office, a full-time director, and a small staff. One of its main functions has been to procure inputs and consumer goods nationally and internationally, and deliver them to regional warehouses and cooperative outlets in rural areas. Another has been to help small producers organize their own cooperative stores. It also helps the local and departmental supply commissions that guide operations in each cooperative store and establishes pricing policies within regional and national guidelines.

In areas where an ECODEPA cooperative store has been established, all small farmers are eligible to purchase supplies. Members may receive a discount, but they must make a financial contribution, in relation to their financial position, to the cooperative's capital. Each member has only one vote in the cooperative assembly, regardless of the size of their investment. As a rule all purchases are made in cash, and sufficient margins are required to ensure that the cooperative stores can be self-financing.

ECODEPA has a policy requiring that each *Tienda Campesina* be fully organized before it can receive supplies and begin selling them to small farmers. There should be a regional ECODEPA supply commission, and a director, warehouse, and transport system. A local supply commission must also be in place and priorities set. The cooperative should be fully equipped with bye-laws, and have a formal procedure for electing its president, directors and committees. There should be suitable buildings to store and sell the supplies. A book keeping system should be set up, and an accountant or book keeper trained. Only once members of the cooperative have contributed to initial working capital, will ECODEPA begin to furnish the store with goods.

By December 1986 about 120 cooperative stores had been formed in this way and were in operation. Several dozen more were being scheduled to begin functioning in 1987.

The initial stock of goods in each store, which until mid-1986 was purchased almost entirely with funds from Sweden, acts as the initial capital of the *Tiendas Campesinas*. All replenishments, however, must be paid for in full, and in cash (in local currency). This provides ECODEPA with a permanent revolving fund to continue autonomous operations. The system implies an obligation on the part of the government to exchange ECODEPA's local currency at some agreed-upon exchange rate, as ECODEPA must depend upon imported supplies to replenish its initial stock.

A visit to the Matagalpa regional warehouse in December 1986, and to a *Tienda Campesina* in San Dionisio in May 1986 revealed a brisk business with rapid turnover. The warehouse had boots from Guatemala, files from Sweden, cooking utensils from China, barbed wire from Colombia, machetes from El Salvador and many other vital items for peasant farmers.The *Tienda* was selling boots, herbicides, and machetes to dozens of peasants, who arrived on foot, horse or mule, even on a Sunday morning.

ECODEPA's first priority continues to be getting vital supplies to peasants in those zones most affected by the war. It does not attempt to compete with state agencies, but to supplement their work. It also tries to resist peasant pressure to expand more rapidly than is permitted by its capacity to obtain and distribute supplies, or to train the necessary accountants, book keepers, and cooperative leadership. Where it has not been able to restrain expansion, the valuable training has been sacrificed, serving as a lesson for the whole of ECODEPA. While it hopes eventually to play an important role in marketing small farmers' produce, it concentrates primarily on improving their access to required inputs and vital consumer goods.

During 1985 and 1986 ECODEPA imported about $4 million worth of supplies. About 12 percent of these imports were for the enterprise's trucks, office equipment, and office supplies; and 8 percent were for things like spare parts, tyres and batteries to maintain farmers' vehicles and other machinery. The remaining $3 million was spent partly on basic farming tools such as machetes, hoes, axes, shovels, hammers, nails and wire; and partly on basic goods required by rural households such as rubber boots, cloth, kitchen utensils, kerosene lamps, zinc roofing, and knives. These supplies were purchased primarily from Guatemala, El Salvador, Costa Rica, Colombia, Mexico, China and Taiwan, although some came from Sweden and other European sources. Only aspirin tablets, the export of which is not prohibited by the blockade, came from the United States.

ECODEPA has had serious problems in the course of its rapid expansion. The biggest, aside from the havoc caused by Contra aggression, was the difficulty in getting supplies. The demand was so much greater than the relatively small quantity it has been able to import or procure locally, that peasant demands remain unfulfilled. Nicaragua's underdeveloped industrial sector has never had the capacity to produce for small farmers' needs, as more profits were to be made serving agro-industry, manufacturing for export or urban markets. This supply problem is compounded by transport difficulties. ECODEPA and UNAG have few vehicles, and must frequently rely on leasing or contracting from private truckers and traders. Vehicles are frequently immobilized as spare parts are scarce and must be imported.

Other problems have been caused by inflation and by the government's pricing policy. Prices were frequently set too low to permit a good return on peasants' products. This has been aggravated by inflation, which has been accelerated by the war and reached over 700 percent per year by late 1986.

Multiple official foreign exchange rates, plus parallel and black-market ones, also make financial control and planning exceedingly difficult. Margins of 5, 10 or even 15 percent are charged for each transaction to cover costs. There is a margin for moving imported supplies from the port of entry to the regional warehouse, another margin for delivery from the warehouse to the store and another on final sale. With a stable currency these would be more than adequate. With rapid inflation, however, it becomes imperative to convert cash into goods immediately if a cooperative's margins are not to become negative in real terms, leading to a loss of capital in the enterprise. Moreover, it takes some time to train cooperative leaders, accountants, clerks, and book keepers in rural areas—where levels of literacy were extremely low before the revolution.

Swedish aid to UNAG has been absolutely crucial in getting ECODEPA off the ground. The Swedish emergency fund donations made it possible for ECODEPA to import the initial supplies that were unavailable in Nicaragua. Equally important has been the technical assistance provided by the CCS. Several Swedish cooperative specialists have been working constantly with the ECODEPA leadership in Managua and regionally, as well as with many local *Tiendas Campesinas*. Their assistance has been vital in arranging for imports, setting up organizational guidelines, and helping to design financial and inventory control systems. Also, most of these technicians and professionals had experience working with farmers'cooperatives in Sweden, and some had been farmers themselves. This made their assistance particularly valuable for ECODEPA and UNAG.

ECODEPA's operating costs have been extremely low. Much of the work is done by the cooperative members and there are few salaried workers or other overhead costs. Where ECODEPA has been able to purchase produce from small-scale farmers, it has often been able to pay better prices than private traders, and sell to consumers at far lower prices than those prevailing in urban markets.

The short-term future for ECODEPA looks promising. Support from aid agencies is increasing, and active participation by peasant producers contributes to its success. The state has also gradually become more supportive. Initially, several government agencies were critical of UNAG's new role. Some considered it an unnecessary duplication of state marketing functions, while others were concerned that by concentrating human resources on setting up the new distribution network, UNAG was neglecting its primary roles in peasant mobilization and cooperative organization. The experience of the past two years, however, has shown that ECODEPA's activities complement rather than duplicate those of the state, and that the UNAG enterprises are more responsive to the small-scale farmer's needs than government marketing agencies. The second concern, over UNAG's role as peasant mobilizer and cooperative organizer, reflected a more real problem: but one that was to be expected during the initial phase, when peasant stores were being set up throughout the country. This concern was possibly short-sighted, however, for UNAG's capacity to mobilize and organize was likely to increase if small producers saw their interests being directly supported by the organization.

As ECODEPA gains experience and improves its organizational and economic capacity, it could become a major instrument, controlled by Nicaragua's small-scale farmers, in supplying rural families with essential products, and strengthening the mixed economy. ECODEPA is of course, highly vulnerable to reductions in aid, and its long-term success will depend on the capacity of the Nicaraguan economy to generate export revenues, expand light industry, and develop new forms of cooperation and trade with other Central American countries.

'SCHOOLS IN THE VALLEYS' One of the hallmarks of the Sandinista revolution has been the rapid expansion of education services. Between 1978 and 1984 the total student population more than doubled—from 533,000 to 1,167,000. This represented an increase from 20 to 37 percent of the total population. Aid from Western Europe and North America has made an important contribution in this area. NGOs and solidarity groups have been particularly active in building schools and obtaining materials. For these reasons it was important to include an education project in our assessment.'Schools in the Valleys' is an ambitious school construction project, begun in 1980 with funding from the NGO SWISSAID and the Swiss government. Its aim is to increase access to education in rural areas neglected before the revolution. In building the schools, the project has also sought to develop community participation, use local resources, and establish a decentralized management.

The project is directed by Grupo Sofonias, an international team that develops projects and acts as counsel and technical adviser to existing projects, on the invitation of local organizations. Established in 1979, Grupo Sofonias is composed of two Guatemalan educators, a Swiss architect, a Canadian political scientist, and three Nicaraguans. The schools project is an example of the innovative, flexible project implementation, which Grupo Sofonias calls 'base-focused development'. It illustrates many of the common difficulties development organizations have experienced in the course of rapidly changing social and economic conditions.

The project's first school, in the municipality of San Juan del Sur in the southern Pacific Coast region, was built by Grupo Sofonias and the Ministry of Education. It led to requests for schools from several other villages in the municipality. The subsequent construction of six new classrooms then provoked an avalanche of requests from others. Within 3 years, 70 new classrooms had been completed in 40 villages, and improvements made to 20 more in 10 other villages. In the next 3 years, the project was extended to the departments of Carazo, Granada and Masaya, and 96 more classrooms built or improved, taking 3 to 4 months for the construction of one classroom. External financing for the project over the six years has amounted to about $1.4 million.

In the project, the community itself must take the initiative and approach the Ministry of Education, rather than have the government impose its choice on a community. The Ministry of Education, in consultation with Grupo Sofonias, then decides whether or not to build the school, given constraints on finances and human resources, and the number of other classrooms under construction. The communities are required to demonstrate willingness by carrying out preparatory work—gathering stones or digging holes. The community then provides voluntary labour: in construction, providing meals for labourers, and organizing fundraising activities. The community also manages a rotating fund to purchase local materials, and maintain and improve the schools when they are finished. In building the schools,

> "Involvement of the community is viewed by all three parties as a fundamental social component so that the schools are not perceived as a gift, neither from the Ministry of Education, nor from Grupo Sofonias nor SWISSAID. People working together get to know one another in new ways and their involvement contributes to the development of a commitment to see something through, from its initiation to maintenance of the finished work. Thus, the schoolhouse truly becomes of the community."[13]

The most common problem of community participation has been a scarcity of helpers for the masons. The need for labour in agriculture results in a suspension of construction during peak seasons. Other activities such as adult education, and conscription, have also drawn people away. Another initially limiting factor—mistrust due to the unfulfilled promises of the past—lessened as Grupo Sofonias and the Ministry of Education honoured their commitments, and people saw more and more schools being built.

Participants expressed pride in their accomplishment, their ability to overcome difficulties, their maintenance of the new schools, and in the fact that many schools had become community centres for vaccination campaigns, adult education, and meetings of cooperatives, religious groups and parents' associations. Encouraging members of the community to work together clearly contributed to the commitment and responsibility of participants and to the development of leadership and organizational skills.

The project has used local resources wherever possible, including skilled and unskilled labour for construction and supervision, and local materials such as stone, lime, brick, and roofing substances like fibralix. The emphasis on local resources was partly a result of the difficulty of transporting materials to remote areas. Many villages are reached only by dirt roads and become totally cut off during the rainy season. Another reason for using local resources was to minimize imports and "help free [foreign] exchange for other socially beneficial commodities", and because "the use of paid local skilled labour contributes to the circulation of money at the local level, which is an essential ingredient for the economic health of a community or region''.[14] Using local resources also stimulates the local economy, introduces techniques the inhabitants themselves can follow, and lowers total costs. The cost of the classrooms built in this project has been half the conventional cost calculated by the Ministry of Education.

However, the project's departure from conventional construction techniques has also created problems. Rooves were made of wood and tiles instead of imported tin. Then scarcity of wood led to the development of the fibre-cement material fibralix, which also substituted asbestos-cement, and cut the cost of imported components by one third. But fibralix is a new material: its durability is uncertain, and its components have become increasingly difficult to find. The project has therefore experimented with arched brick rooves not requiring wood. The innovative techniques met with resistance at first. Some people preferred tin rooves, or they expected the more elaborate type of school they had seen in towns. These problems were gradually solved through explanation and discussion. Moreover, as the project intended, community members have gone on to use the new techniques to repair or build their own houses, and, in one case, a restaurant.

A final objective of the project has been decentralized or 'appropriate management', meaning giving responsibility to many people, conducting the project primarily on site, and minimizing administration. The project director works and lives locally, is attuned to events in the area and to the progress of the project by participating in it and being part of the community. Together with a decentralized and mobile administration, this helps to overcome communication problems—which are often severe due to the lack of transport and the absence of a telephone. Grupo Sofonias also sees its relationship with the Ministry of Education as decentralized and based on mutual trust, and notes the government's openness to alternatives: ''They give us a lot of freedom; we don't have to ask for authorization for every little thing''.

This project has been more directly affected by the war than most others surveyed in this chapter. During the construction of one school close to the Costa Rican border, the masons refused to continue working after death threats from the Contras, and the school had to be finished with the help of the Sandinista youth organization. Later, this school and four others in the narrow strip between the Lake of Nicaragua and the border were forced to close when the area was evacuated in 1982. In the last two years, increasing difficulties in obtaining both labour and materials have forced the project to devote more resources to repairing and improving existing schools than to building new ones. More recently, teachers have also been in short supply since low state salaries lead them to prefer work in the informal or private sectors.

Despite these difficulties, the project directors' evaluation of the project and the members of Grupo Sofonias we interviewed attributed the success of the project largely to the social conditions brought about by the revolution, which promote popular participation, increase the demand for education, and permit a unity of purpose between Grupo Sofonias and the Ministry of Education.[15]

PESTICIDE HEALTH AND SAFETY PROGRAMME

From the 1950s onwards Nicaragua experienced a cotton boom. In the years leading up to the revolution, the area sown in cotton accounted for as much as 30 percent of the total crop area. As cotton production expanded rapidly, so too did the use of imported pesticides. By 1965 Nicaragua was importing over 19 million kilograms of insecticide at a cost of over $10 million per year, of which 87 percent was being used in cotton production.[16] Moreover, after 1967, Somoza allowed multinational corporations to test uncertified chemicals in Nicaragua at a cost of $1,000 per chemical at the Cotton Experimental Centre in Posoltega. Compounds such as endrin, dieldrin, kepone, leptophos, lindane and DDT were still being used in Nicaragua in the 1970s when they had been restricted or banned in the United States. Acute pesticide poisonings among Nicaraguan farm workers reached more than 3,000 annually between 1962 and 1972, or eight times their incidence in the United States.[17] Pesticide-related illness and death among farmers and agricultural labourers has been among the highest in the world. Even as recently as 1980, human tissue samples in Nicaragua still carried 16 times the global average DDT burden.[18] Furthermore, these pesticides permitted only short-lived increases in yields, since insects developed a resistance to them; at the same time, they devastated the insects' natural predators.

In response to this situation, the post-revolutionary government instituted reforms to reduce the poisonings and environmental contamination caused by excessive and careless pesticide application over the short term, and over the long term, to reduce the use of expensive and highly toxic pesticides.

The Pesticide Health and Safety Programme was begun in 1985 as part of this effort. It is administered by CARE Nicaragua, [19] and external support has been provided by the American Friends Service Committee,

Catholic Relief Services, CARE USA, Development and Peace of Canada, Oxfam Canada, and the General Mills Corporation. Total costs amounted to $300,778 over the first two years, with another $400,000 to be raised for the next two years.

The programme has 6 staff who work with representatives from the agricultural and industrial workers unions (ATC and CST), the ministries of labour (MITRAB), health (MINSA), agrarian reform (MIDINRA), and education (MED), as well as the Institute of the Environment and Natural Resources (IRENA). The programme focuses on pesticide poisoning around León and Chinandega where most of Nicaragua's cotton is produced, addressing health and safety in the workplace, illness-monitoring and emergency alert, and training and education.

The health and safety project focuses on high-risk workplaces, namely the airfields where concentrated chemicals are mixed and loaded into spray planes. This was traditionally done by hand with plastic buckets, and often without proper protective equipment. Even a small amount of the most commonly used chemical, methyl parathion, is potentially lethal if it touches the skin, and in 1985 it resulted in 18 deaths in the project area alone. To prevent spillage and exposure to the substance, the project is installing 'closed systems' of pumps and siphons leading directly from the chemical barrels into the airplane's spray tank, which mix the chemical with the correct amount of water. Within the first year, the project fitted 20 of the 75 airstrips in the region with closed systems, and planned to install another 10. Additional closed systems have been bought privately, and the government is closing down unequipped airstrips on safety grounds. Workplaces are also being paved with cement and fitted with a filter system to prevent the underground water from becoming poisoned with chemical run-off, and personnel are being provided with protective clothing and respiratory equipment.

The illness-monitoring and emergency alert project seeks to give 5,000 people regular check-ups during the pesticide-spraying season. A simple illness-monitoring test, with a blood sample and questionnaire, can detect poisoning before the worker experiences symptoms. People whose test results are positive are immediately informed and taken off the job. They are entitled to most of their salary and are re-checked a week later before being allowed to return to work. The project provides a doctor for serious cases. In addition, an emergency response team has been set up in the Ministry of Health to prevent potential disasters. For example, when old pesticide-treated seed corn was taken from a dump by local residents the response team was able to reach them before they ate the corn: in many parts of the world similar events have killed hundreds.

Training is given to farmers from both state and private farms in conjunction with MITRAB, MINSA, MIDINRA and the ATC. Ministry officials are also trained: for example, in carrying out weekly site visits to ensure proper use and maintenance of the 'closed systems', or in inspecting work sites to ensure adherence to the new safety code. A pesticide health expert has been brought in to train medical students and doctors to identify and treat pesticide illness. Computerized data-gathering has also been set up to identify high-risk workplaces and provide data for policy-making. Thus, training is extended beyond the immediate tasks, to achieve a wider level of general competence. As the project director put it: "In attempting to solve a technical problem, we have had to train people to become better managers; we've taught them how to become better administrators, how to use a computer, and how to deal with foreign funders."

The community education segment of the programme addresses the widespread ignorance of pesticide hazards and safety measures in rural areas. Abandoned pesticide barrels are sometimes used for bathing children or storing drinking water. The brown-coloured liquid paraquat, the primary cause of death from pesticides in the Third World in 1983, is often stored in coca-cola bottles in Nicaragua. Whereas inhalation was traditionally believed to be the prime cause of pesticide poisoning, and use of respirators emphasised, in fact two-thirds of pesticide poisonings are caused by dermal absorption. Skin protection and washing had been neglected. More recently, as men have been conscripted into the military, pesticide application is increasingly handled by women and children. Children and unborn foetuses are more at risk since pesticides affect the unmatured nervous system, and can cause birth defects, learning disorders, and damage to the immune system.

To raise awareness of these dangers, and promote preventive measures, the project produces educational materials, radio programmes and local newspaper and magazine articles. Health service teams conduct educational activities in the rural communities, and theatre groups and musicians have also been used. Guidelines have been drawn up to include pesticide health and safety in school curricula starting in 1987.

The difficulties experienced in the project are similar to those faced by other development efforts in Nicaragua. The purchase and distribution of imported components has been delayed by bureaucratic problems and bottlenecks at customs offices. European suppliers have had to be found to replace previous U.S. suppliers of vehicles, computers, and other manufactured items; European spare parts have furthermore often been incompatible with U.S. ones, forcing the original equipment to be abandoned. Nicaraguan contributions to the project have been devalued by inflation, and dollar contributions have lost value as the dollar declined on international currency markets. The project has also been impeded by the high turnover of ministry officials.

There have also been problems of coordination among the four ministries involved. These were more acute at the central level than in the cotton-growing regions where officials were aware of the seriousness of pesticide problems. Pressure had to be exerted to involve health-care personnel in decisions about pesticide regulation, which were previously based on agricultural and economic grounds alone. Once, in order to convince one uncooperative ministry official, workers involved in the project joined in a weekly television programme in which citizens voice their complaints directly to ministers and the president himself. The project director saw this as an instance of increasing flexibility and responsiveness within Nicaraguan bureaucracy: "In the last year there has been a real recognition within the government of over-bureaucratization as a serious problem, and this has resulted in a significant policy shift towards the regionalization of authority and towards the interests of the unions and mass organizations." He also noted that "the Nicaraguan government has demonstrated a level of cooperation with donors and project administrators that no other government in Latin America can match."

From mid-1988, when the infrastructure is in place, the project should be sustained with local resources alone, and CARE will sharply reduce its contribution. The programme will be used as a model for a much larger-scale effort to address the pesticide problem not only in the rest of Nicaragua, but in other parts of the world, notably Zimbabwe, Ecuador and Costa Rica. After visiting the project, other Latin American countries have asked for similar programmes. The chairman of the Swedish National Board of Occupational Health concluded that the pesticide programme in Nicaragua could serve as the basis for a long-term regional occupational health programme, with León as the centre of pesticide health research for all of Latin America. The project has thus been successful not only in addressing the pesticide problem in Nicaragua, but also in raising international awareness and proposing viable alternatives for other Third World countries.

VIDEONIC

Videonic is a video training and production centre in Managua. Begun in 1984 as a four-year project, it was the first educational video facility to exist in Nicaragua. Its objective has been to train young Nicaraguans to use video equipment, and to produce images of contemporary Nicaragua which challenge distortions in the view of the country presented by the international news agencies. After two years the project has not only produced high-quality material, but it has also become self-financing. It has therefore been possible to initiate a sequel: the Videoteca project, consisting of an archive, and a screening and promotion centre for Nicaraguan video.

Videonic has been supported by 15 development organizations from Europe: Oxfam 'U.K.', Christian Aid, the Catholic Fund for Overseas Development, Trocaire, Evangelisches Missionswerk, CEBEMO, Vastenaktie, and Oxfam Belgium; from Canada, Development and Peace, Cansave, Oxfam Canada, Interpares, and United Church of Canada; and from the United States, National Council of Churches, and the United Methodist Church. By the end of 1986, these agencies had contributed $166,000.

The project grew out of the success of films on post-revolutionary Nicaragua produced by its two directors, who are film makers from Britain and Chile. These antecedents included examinations of the role of the Catholic Church in the revolutionary process, of the Nicaraguan penitentiary system, and a film about the first woman member of the FSLN to go to the guerilla war in the mountains.

In its first two years, an administrative office and an editing workshop were designed and built, a production studio equipped with top-quality video broadcast technology, and six young persons—three men and three women—trained in producing documentary videos on national affairs for foreign distribution. The trainees are committed to completing the three-year course, staying at Videonic a further three years, and then taking over direction of the project.

The course consists of 6 months of administrative and technical training, including intensive English, photography, history of Latin American literature, film theory and appreciation, film techniques and location filming and recording. This preparation permits the students to provide professional services in photography, research and pre-production work, camera assistance, sound recording, editing assistance, and the transfer of videos to different formats. Further training advances them to apprenticeship in camera use, sound, editing, production, direction, subtitling and computerized archive systems. The final stage consists of on-site experience and full production of videos under the supervision of instructors.

Four documentaries were made in Videonic's first two years. *The Other Invasion* (1984) covers achievements in health care since the revolution, and the impact of the war on the Nicaraguan health system. This film was later promoted in the United States in a bilingual public television series broadcast across the country. In San Francisco, this raised $4,000 for health projects in Nicaragua. *Nicaraguan Journey* (1984) documents a European Women's Peace Delegation to Nicaragua, drawing links between peace and women's movements in the United States and Europe, and the struggle for peace in Central America. *Development Under Fire* (1986), sponsored by Christian Aid, CAFOD, War on Want, and Oxfam 'U.K.', focuses on the effects of economic destabilization in Nicaragua. *In the Shadow of War* (1986), narrated by Glenda Jackson and sponsored by Christian Aid, demonstrates the importance of NGO aid in the Nicaraguan economy and the role of the Protestant Church in channelling aid. Of the highest quality in the country, these documentaries have been well received abroad, and are widely used by educational institutions, trade unions, and church and solidarity groups. A recently completed fifth film on the participation of women in the democratic process in Nicaragua received a Special Mention at the Havana Film Festival in December 1986. Entitled *Son Nicas*, it focuses on two women elected to the National Assembly, an ex-nun and a mother of a 15-year-old girl who was murdered by Somoza's National Guard. New videos in progress look at the indigenous communities on the Atlantic Coast (financed by NOVIB and VARA TV in the Netherlands), education, and disabled victims of the war.

The students are enthusiastic about the course: "We never thought we'd have this opportunity in Nicaragua. The equipment we use is of the same quality as that of any developed country." They point out the readiness with which they were given responsibility and creative freedom, whereas "In England, for example, after spending 3 years in film school, the students have to spend years as camera assistants before they are permitted to take charge of the equipment and have a significant role in production." Another advantage of the training programme was its sexual equality. "In other countries it is rare to see women who are given the job of director. Here we are all equal." Through Videonic, they also had the opportunity to meet many interesting people who pass through Nicaragua.

The difficulties confronting the project tend to be external, and are of a bureaucratic or economic nature, as in many other projects in Nicaragua. These are:

- problems with importing equipment, office supplies, and so on, due to customs bureaucracy;
- poor availability of imported spare parts, due to the country's lack of foreign exchange;

- inflation, which outstrips the official exchange rate, so that a proportion of the funds obtained are lost.

The fact that the project has become self-financing after two years, is one of its major successes. This has been achieved primarily by co-producing documentaries with other organizations, and by hiring out services to foreign film producers in Nicaragua. These filming, editing and production services have been provided to the National Council of Churches (United States), the Metropolitan Conference of the Methodist Churches (United States), and television networks such as the BBC, CBC, PBS, the National Film Board of Canada, Australian TV, Denmark Radio, and Dutch VARA TV.

As a result of its self-financing status, Videonic has been able to offer numerous free services to religious, student, and mass organizations in Nicaragua, further contributing to the development of cultural activities and visual information in the country. Videoteca was set up to promote research and educational use of video more effectively. Upon completion it will provide a 70-seat theatre for 16mm video projection, a small projecting room, a recording and copying room, a graphic design workshop, a photographic darkroom, a café, and an archive of national productions, foreign productions on Nicaragua, and film classics not previously available in Nicaragua. In the past, the lack of facilities for collecting, reproducing, and screening new material led to underuse of the flourishing video output since the revolution—not only in Videonic, but also at INCINE, the Ministry of Agricultural Development and Agrarian Reform, and the trade unions' (CST-ATC) Popular Video Workshop. Videoteca started in February 1986 with the support of one Dutch and 2 British agencies.

Videonic shows how a relatively small amount of aid can open up a whole new area in communications, which previously did not exist. As one of the project directors pointed out: "The cost of financing the whole project, including the employment of 16 people for 2 years is [no more than] the cost of making 2 full-length documentary films." Given the project's emphasis on training, the transfer of skills to operate the relatively sophisticated equipment has not proved a major problem—as is often the case in projects of this nature. Also, since the project is able to generate foreign exchange, its economic future seems fairly secure. As such it seems that Videonic has managed to avoid several of the pitfalls commonly associated with projects involving the transfer of capital-intensive technologies to developing countries.

PRINCIPAL PROBLEMS IN PROJECT IMPLEMENTATION

The projects reviewed above highlight some of the major problems in project implementation. These are summarized below.

1. SIZE AND LOCATION

The size of a project determines to a significant extent the ease with which it can be implemented. Problems in ensuring adequate planning, coordination, administration, supplies of materials, inputs, human resources, and financing, all increase exponentially with a project's magnitude.

Of the five projects assessed in this report, only Chiltepe could be considered large, in its total use of resources, and capital-intensive imported technologies. It experienced considerable delays due to insufficient capacity to build roads and buildings. Videonic is capital-intensive but very small. ECODEPA covers a wide geographical area, and involves a large number of people: but has so far had modest requirements for external resources. ECODEPA and the schools project experienced the most direct difficulties from the war as they were sometimes located near the borders. The other projects operated in more secure areas. Indeed, ECODEPA was created partly in response to supply-problems in regions suffering from Contra incursions. The schools project has so far involved the construction of 186 classrooms, made with little use of external resources, and emphasising the use of 'appropriate technologies' and local personnel and materials. The pesticide project has modest requirements for imported technology.

2. LABOUR SHORTAGES

Inadequate skilled and unskilled labour affected the implementation of all five projects to some extent, but was most serious for Chiltepe. The project is large and involves skill-demanding technology—and the original plans failed to allow for adequate training. Chiltepe also sometimes had difficulty finding and keeping enough unskilled labourers. Wages did not keep pace with inflation, and the shortage of consumer goods made work in the informal sector in Managua attractive. The war meant conscription of many labourers, both skilled and unskilled. Even the small Videonic project had a temporary setback when a key technician was called up.

Chiltepe has dealt with the 'manpower' problem by encouraging women from surrounding communities and urban centres to work on the project, and increasing fringe-benefits through the installation of an irrigated garden area, where workers can produce their own food. ECODEPA has put priority on the training of locally recruited accountants and administrators, as well as peasants, in cooperative organization and procedures. Since cooperative members do most of the work, there is no problem finding unskilled labour. The school construction programme emphasises voluntary labour by the members of each community. But masons and carpenters still had to be trained, and given additional incentives. Videonic and the pesticide safety project are essentially training schemes.

3. PROBLEMS WITH SUPPLIES AND INPUTS

Obtaining supplies, construction materials and inputs is another common problem. Construction companies often lack the capacity to undertake large projects, which partly explains why Chiltepe has run nearly two years behind its original schedule. There are also delays in obtaining necessary inputs, including energy. Frequent blackouts have increased costs.

To avoid delays, ECODEPA set up its own network to receive imported supplies at ports of entry, and for storage, transport and delivery to central, regional and local warehouses. However, both its own vehicles and those it contracted were often put out of operation by the lack of imported spare parts and tyres. The other projects experienced similar difficulties in different degrees.

4. PROBLEMS WITH ADMINISTRATION AND COORDINATION

Numerous problems in project implementation can be attributed to inadequate planning, compounded by lack of experience. Some of the delays were simply unavoidable, however, because of the war, the embargo, the over-strained economy and various events at home or abroad that were not only unforeseen, but essentially unforeseeable.

Another problem frequently encountered was in coordination between ministries and agencies. For example, the pesticide safety project required close cooperation with the Ministries of Health, Labour and Agriculture. This proved difficult at the head offices, but was much more easily arranged locally, where the problems of pesticide poisonings were well recognized. The ECODEPA project ran into initial difficulties because the departments in the Ministries of Agriculture and of Internal Commerce which were responsible for supplying peasants, saw UNAG's initiative as an unnecessary duplication of their effort. This problem was settled satisfactorily through an agreement between UNAG and the respective ministers.

Coordination between different donors supporting the same project proved easier than some observers had anticipated. In practice, cooperation among donors was readily arranged through the Nicaraguan directors of each project. Several NGOs work together in supporting Videonic and the pesticide safety projects. The Swedish government and four NGOs, each from a different country, are supporting ECODEPA financially without friction. Chiltepe has received external resources from two multilateral donors and bilateral sources in Canada, Western Europe and Eastern Europe.

5. FINANCIAL PROBLEMS

All the projects suffered the effects of inflation. In 1986, despite the fact that Chiltepe was producing enough milk for over half Managua's consumers—which would have more than covered its costs at planned prices, its receipts from milk sales were insufficient to meet costs. This was not due to inefficient marketing, but because the official price of milk was held down to benefit low-income consumers. A change in this policy in late 1986 enabled the Chiltepe project to cover current operating costs.

Accelerating inflation has also made ECODEPA's operation extremely difficult. The project tries to be self-supporting by charging peasant buyers cash for their supplies, and taking small fixed profits for each transaction. Rapid inflation has made it almost impossible, however, to convert the cash into goods and services quickly enough to avoid losing all profit through depreciation. Videonic, on the other hand, was able to become self-financing rather quickly, because it sold many of its services and films to foreign clients—who paid in hard currency.

The Chiltepe project illustrates another deeper problem inherent in most capital-intensive large-scale investments, which are designed to save foreign exchange either by increasing exports or, in this case, reducing imports. Nicaragua's small industrial base cannot produce the spare parts needed by most imported machinery. Yearly imports of about $100,000 in goods will be required to cover depreciation, and keep the Chiltepe project in operation. Its growing need of feed-concentrates and fodder will also increase demands on foreign exchange. Because the project's returns come in local currency, the government will have to allocate scarce foreign exchange to keep it operating. A further problem for Chiltepe is that powdered milk is currently in surplus on world markets, and can be easily obtained by donation. Under these conditions, little foreign exchange will actually be saved by substituting the Nicaraguan milk for donated or low-priced imported milk.

Despite these problems there was a fair consensus among the donor agency representatives and government and project personnel we interviewed that the projects were a relative success—bearing in mind prevailing economic constraints and the war. These, and hundreds of other projects being implemented in Nicaragua, were clearly helping Nicaragua fulfil the fundamental development goals of meeting basic needs, and working towards popular participation and longer-term self reliance.

However, considerable scope for improved use of external resources remains, in three major areas. Unnecessary delays by the government in disbursing funds, distributing materials and accounting for the use of aid must be overcome, in order to accelerate project implementation and retain the confidence of donors. More resources need to go to projects which strengthen the mixed economy by supporting individual peasant producers, rural and urban cooperatives, and private producers. Present crisis conditions demand more emphasis on quick-yielding rather than slow-yielding projects.

Recent economic plans and policy statements indicate that the Nicaraguan government has taken stock of the situation and is attempting to move in these directions. This has been partly a response to pressure from donors, but is primarily due to the the current crisis: the root cause of which is the war. But signing a peace agreement would not end the crisis. Hundreds of thousands of people need to be relocated, re-housed and re-employed. The economy has been seriously dislocated—and shortages of foreign exchange will remain a major constraint on development. The recovery process will take years—and the type of policy changes and development initiatives introduced recently must be sustained. Western aid has a crucial role to play in guaranteeing the success of these initiatives.

Notes to Chapter 4

1. D. Melrose, *Nicaragua: The Threat of A Good Example*, Oxfam Public Affairs Unit, Oxfam, Oxford, U.K., 1985, pp. 6-7.
2. Ibid., p. 1.
3. World Council of Churches, *Report on Nicaragua*; quoted in D. Melrose, op. cit., p. 12.
4. Authors' interview, Managua, November 1986.
5. IDB, "Report No. DES-13", Nicaragua, January 1983; quoted in D. Melrose, op. cit., p. 26.
6. Authors' interview, Managua, November 1986.
7. Ibid.
8. Ibid.
9. Ibid.
10. Ibid.
11. See M.O. Colin, "La Problemática de la Cooperación Internacional a Nicaragua", paper presented at the Fifth Congress of Nicaraguan Social Scientists, Managua, October 1986.
12. *Barricada*, 7 July, 1986.
13. "Schools in the Valleys", evaluation for SWISSAID, 1983, p. 6.
14. Ibid., p. 6.
15. Ibid., p. 100.
16. S. Sweezy, D. Murray, and R. Daxl, "Nicaragua's Revolution in Pesticide Policy", *Environment*, vol. 28, no. 1, January/February 1986, p. 8.
17. Ibid., p. 29.
18. Ibid.
19. CARE is an international aid and relief agency. Care Nicaragua is supported primarily by CARE Canada and CARE Norway. Additional funds are also provided by CARE USA and the Dutch government through CARE International.

ABBREVIATIONS

AMNLAE	Asociación de Mujeres Nicaragüenses Luisa Amanda Espinoza; Luisa Amanda Espinoza Association of Nicaraguan Women.
ANDEN	Asociación Nacional de Educadores Nicaragüenses; National Association of Nicaraguan Teachers.
ANS	Asociación de Niños Sandinistas; Association of Sandinista Children.
ASTC	Asociación Sandinista de Trabajadores de la Cultura; Sandinista Association of Cultural Workers.
ATC	Asociación de Trabajadores del Campo; Association of Farm Workers.
BCIE	Banco Centroamericana de Integración Económica; Central American Bank of Economic Integration.
CDS	Comité de Defensa Sandinista; Sandinista Defence Committee.
CAFOD	Catholic Fund for Overseas Development.
CCS	Swedish Cooperative Centre.
CEBEMO	Catholic Organization for Joint Financing of Develop ment Programmes (Netherlands).
CEPAD	Comité Evangélico Pro-Ayuda al Desarollo; Evangelical Committee for Development Aid.
CIDA	Canadian International Development Agency.
CIERA	Centro de Investigaciones y Estudios de la Reforma Agraria; Centre for Research and Studies on Agrarian Reform.
COMECON	Council for Mutual Economic Assistance.
CONARCA	Comisión Nacional para la Renovación de los Cafetales; National Commission for Coffee Renovation.
CST	Central Sandinista de Trabajadores; Sandinista Union of Workers.
DEH	Swiss Ministry of Development Cooperation.
ECLAC	Economic Commission for Latin America and the Caribbean.
ECODEPA	Empresa Cooperativa de Productores Agropecuarios; Agricultural Producers Cooperative.

ENABAS	Empresa Nicaragüense de Alimentos Básicos; Nicaraguan Basic Food Enterprise.
FACS	Fundación Augusto César Sandino; Augusto César Sandino Foundation.
FAO	Food and Agriculture Organization.
FETSALUD	Federación de Trabajadores de la Salud; Federation of Health Workers.
FINAPRI	Fondo de Inversiones y Preinversiones; Investment Fund.
FIR	Fondo International de Reconstrucción; International Reconstruction Fund.
HIVOS	Humanistic Institute for Development Cooperation (Netherlands).
IBRD	International Bank for Reconstruction and Development (World Bank).
IDB	Inter-American Development Bank.
IFAD	International Fund for Agricultural Development.
IMF	International Monetary Fund.
INAA	Instituto Nicaragüense de Acueductos y Alcantarillados; Nicaraguan Water and Sewage Institute.
INCINE	Instituto Nicaragüense del Cine; Nicaraguan Film Institute.
INE	Instituto Nicaragüense de Energía; Nicaraguan Energy Institute.
INETER	Instituto Nicaragüense de Estudios Territoriales; Nicaraguan Territorial Institute.
INMINE	Instituto Nicaragüense de Minería; Nicaraguan Mining Institute.
INNICA	Instituto Nicaragüense de la Costa Atlántica; Nicaraguan Institute of the Atlantic Coast.
INPESCA	Instituto Nicaragüense de la Pesca; Nicaraguan Fishing Institute.
IRENA	Instituto de Recursos Naturales; Institute of Natural Resources.
INSSBI	Instituto Nicaragüense de Seguridad Social y Bienestar; Nicaraguan Institute of Social Security and Welfare.
JRM	Junta de Reconstrucción de Managua; Junta for the Reconstruction of Managua.
JS19J	Juventud Sandinista 19 de Julio; Sandinista Youth Organization.
MCE	Ministerio de Cooperación Externa; Ministry of External Cooperation.

MED	Ministerio de Educación; Ministry of Education.
MICE	Ministerio de Comercio Exterior; Ministry of Foreign Trade.
MICOIN	Ministerio de Comercio Interior; Ministry of Internal Trade.
MICONS	Ministerio de Construcción; Ministry of Construction.
MIDINRA	Ministerio de Desarrollo Agropecuario y Reforma Agraria; Ministry of Agricultural Development and Agrarian Reform.
MIND	Ministerio de Industria; Ministry of Industry.
MINSA	Ministerio de Salud; Ministry of Health.
MIPLAN	Ministerio de Planificación; Ministry of Planning.
MITRANS	Ministerio de Transporte; Ministry of Transport.
NOVIB	Dutch Organization for International Development Cooperation.
OECD	Organization for Economic Cooperation and Development.
PAN	Programa Alimentario Nicaragüense; Nicaraguan Food Program.
SAMU	Secretaría de Asuntos Municipales; Secretariat of Municipal Affaires.
SAR	Sociedad Anónima Regional; Regional Development Enterprise.
SI	Socialist International.
SIDA	Swedish International Development Authority.
SINACAP	Sistema Nacional de Capacitación Profesional; National Professional Training Programme.
SINAFORP	Sistema Nacional de Formación Profesional; National Professional Training Scheme.
SWISSAID	Swiss Foundation for Cooperation and Development.
UCA	Universidad Centroamericana; Central American University (Managua, Nicaragua).
U.N./UNO	United Nations Organization.
UNAG	Unión Nacional de Agricultores y Ganaderos; National Union of Farmers and Cattlemen.
UNDP	United Nations Development Programme.
UNHCR	Office of the United Nations High Commissioner for Refugees.
UNICEF	United Nations Children's Fund.
WFP	World Food Programme.
WHO	World Health Organization.

APPENDIX I: REPRESENTATIVES OF INSTITUTIONS AND AID AGENCIES INTERVIEWED IN NICARAGUA

REPRESENTATIVES OF INSTITUTIONS AND AID AGENCIES INTERVIEWED IN NICARAGUA

Institution	Name
Bilateral Agencies:	
Swedish International Development Agency (SIDA)	M.E. Blanco, E. Holm de Halkjaer
Norwegian Agency for Development	N. Vogt
Office of Dutch Cooperation	G. Bos, M. Haansandts
Canadian International Development Agency (CIDA)	R. Laurence
West German Cooperation Service	E. Susdorf
Non-governmental Organizations:	
Arbeiterhilfswerk (Switzerland)	O. Berthoud
Oxfam Belgium	S. Declercq
Oxfam 'UK'	G. Salinas
CEPAD (Nicaragua)	G. Aguirre
Cansave (Canada)	J. Gunn
Christian Aid (UK)	M. Bailey
Christian Aid (UK)	S. Tickell
Catholic Institute for International Relations (UK)	A. Burge
Multilateral Agencies:	
United Nations	N. Bozen
FAO	K. Blockland
UNICEF	N. García
Nicaraguan Institutions and Agencies:	
Nicaraguan Food Program	J. López, J. Jofre
Ministry of External Cooperation	C. Arce, M.O. Colin
Ministry of Foreign Trade	Ma. R. Renzi
Budget and Planning Office	S.A. Rosales
Augusto César Sandino Foundation	E. Zablah
Office of International Relations and External Cooperation in Matagalpa	M. Jackman
Project Personnel:	
Chiltepe	L. Bárcenas
ECODEPA	B. Kjeller, A. Rivera,
ECODEPA (Matagalpa)	S. Zelaya
Swissaid Schools Project	E. Armira Atz
Videonic	J. Reiter, W. Tirado
Pesticide Health and Safety Programme	D. Murray

APPENDIX II: OVERVIEW OF GRANTS TO NICARAGUA: JULY 1979–JULY 1986

GRANTS TO NICARAGUA: JULY 1979—JULY 1986

(millions of US dollars)

Organization and Country	1979	1980	1981	1982	1983	1984	1985	1986	Total
1. Socialist countries*	—	0.8	4.5	27.3	40.4	68.4	43.5	31.5	216.4
USSR	—	0.4	4.2	26.3	36.3	44.3	12.2	16.3	140.0
Germany, Federal Republic	—	—	—	—	0.6	8.1	10.0	0.2	18.9
Czechoslovakia	—	0.4	0.2	—	—	12.2	0.2	7.4	20.4
Yugoslavia	—	—	—	—	—	—	0.8	1.0	1.8
Cuba	—	—	—	—	—	—	—	0.1	0.1
Hungary	—	—	—	—	0.5	2.1	—	0.4	2.1
Korea	—	—	—	—	1.6	0.1	0.4	—	2.1
Bulgaria	—	—	0.1	1.0	1.4	1.6	13.9	0.5	18.5
Romania	—	—	—	—	—	—	3.2	4.4	7.7
Poland	—	—	—	—	—	—	2.1	0.2	2.3
China	—	—	—	—	—	—	—	1.0	1.0
Vietnam	—	—	—	—	—	—	0.6	—	0.6
2. Western countries and organizations	83.0	79.2	36.7	36.7	36.7	43.0	32.8	16.9	365.0
Western multilateral organizations	9.4	25.3	9.0	14.1	12.7	19.6	13.3	12.8	116.2
UN agencies	2.9	10.0	2.9	8.7	10.1	10.8	10.2	0.5	55.9
UNHCR	2.7	2.2	0.5	0.1	0.2	—	—	—	5.7
UNICEF	0.2	0.9	0.8	6.0	0.9	1.4	2.2	—	12.4
WFP	—	5.2	0.9	2.6	5.6	5.5	2.4	0.5	22.7
FAO	—	1.0	—	—	3.4	0.1	1.3	—	5.8
Other UN agencies	—	0.7	0.7	—	—	3.6	4.3	—	9.3

Western Countries									
Europe									
Austria	0.2	0.5	0.1	0.7	2.2	2.2	0.2	6.1	12.2
Belgium	0.1	0.2	0.4	0.6	0.8	0.6	0.3	—	3.0
Denmark	—	—	1.0	0.1	0.5	0.5	—	—	2.1
Finland	—	—	—	—	0.1	0.9	0.5	—	1.5
France	1.0	0.2	0.7	4.7	2.1	2.1	1.7	2.1	14.6
Germany	2.3	3.2	3.3	1.2	0.5	2.0	0.4	—	12.9
Greece	—	—	—	—	—	—	—	—	N.A.
Ireland	—	0.1	—	—	—	—	—	—	0.1
Italy	0.7	0.3	0.1	0.3	3.2	2.2	0.5	—	7.3
Luxemburg	—	N.A.	N.A.	—	N.A.	—	N.A.	—	N.A.
Netherlands	6.5	6.5	0.5	2.1	3.5	2.9	3.4	—	25.4
Norway	0.3	—	0.4	0.1	0.1	3.1	2.1	—	6.1
Spain	12.2	1.3	—	0.5	0.1	0.9	0.5	0.1	14.1
Sweden	5.8	5.8	3.3	4.7	5.2	3.7	6.5	—	35.0
Switzerland	2.9	0.2	0.7	0.6	0.8	1.3	1.6	—	8.1
United Kingdom	—	0.4	0.6	0.4	0.2	0.1	—	—	1.7

Others:									
Argentina	0.6	—	3.0	3.0	—	1.0	1.7	1.5	10.8
Australia	—	—	—	—	—	—	N.A.	—	N.A.
Canada	1.2	2.7	3.7	2.2	3.3	0.6	0.1	—	13.8
Costa Rica	0.2	—	—	—	—	—	—	—	0.2
Japan	—	2.2	—	0.1	—	—	—	0.1	2.4
Libya	—	—	0.1	—	—	—	—	—	0.1
Mexico	11.8	25.2	5.9	0.4	—	—	—	—	43.3
Panama	10.2	—	—	0.1	—	—	—	—	10.6
Peru	0.3	—	—	—	—	—	—	—	0.3
Taiwan	0.2	—	—	—	—	—	—	—	0.2
USA	15.1	4.2	2.1	1.3	0.2	—	—	—	23.1
Venezuela	1.9	2.2	1.8	—	—	—	—	—	5.9
Other Latin American countries	0.1	—	—	—	—	—	—	—	0.1
TOTAL	**83.0**	**80.0**	**41.2**	**64.0**	**77.1**	**111.4**	**76.3**	**48.4**	**581.4**

* Underestimate.

N.A./ not available.

Source: based on data from the Ministry of External Cooperation.

Appendix III: Destination and Conditions of Medium- and Long-Term Loans from Western Europe and Canada, 19 July 1979–31 December 1985

DESTINATION AND CONDITIONS OF MEDIUM- AND LONG-TERM LOANS FROM WESTERN EUROPE AND CANADA, 19 JULY 1979—31 DECEMBER 1985

(millions of U.S. dollars)

Country/Use	Amount	Grace period (years)	Term (years)	Interest rate (%)	Date signed
WESTERN EUROPE	403.20	—	—	—	—
AUSTRIA	15.10	—	—	—	—
Import of production inputs and consumer goods	6.20	11/10	30	1	11.05.82
Acquisition of consumer goods	6.20	10	30	1	27.09.83
Sack Factory enlargement	1.10	10	30	1	23.05.85
Import of industrial inputs	2.20	10	30	1	23.05.85
DENMARK	7.50	—	—	—	—
Asphalt concrete	3.40	8	17.5	0	29.11.85
Rehabilitation of poultry farms	1.60				1986
Basic grains distribution system	2.50				1986
FINLAND	17.70	—	—	—	—
Purchase of medical equipment	2.50	7.5	25.5	0.75	17.11.81
Electrical and forestry machinery, equipment	3.20	—	—	—	—
Hospital equipment, goods and services	7.40	7.0	25.0	0.75	11.11.84
Rehabilitation of dairy project	4.60	8.0	17.5	0.75	19.12.85
FRANCE	80.60	—	—	—	—
Protocol I	10.00				
Supplies	0.30	6/7.5	17.0	3.50	06.10.80
Miscellaneous	0.70	0.7	7.0	0.50	06.10.80
Consultancies	1.40	—	—		06.10.80
Grain storage	7.60	7.5	17.0	3.50	06.10.80
Protocol II	8.80	—	—	—	—
Import of raw materials	3.50	8.0	25.0	3.50	18.12.81
Import of raw materials	5.30	—	10.0	10.00	18.12.81
Protocol III	14.60	—	—	—	—
Carton factory	8.00	10.5	10/20		16.07.82
Misc. inputs	4.40	10.5	10/20		16.07.82
Irrigation pivots and studies	2.20	10.5	10/20		16.07.82
Protocol IV	15.10	—	—	—	—
Studies	-	10.0	10/30	3	12.09.83
Misc. equipment					
Protocol V	15.50	10.5	20	3	13.06.84
Telecommunications					
Misc. equipment					
Protocol VI	16.60	10.5	20	3	29.03.85
Misc. inputs					
Rehabilitation of industry					
FEDERAL REPUBLIC OF GERMANY	25.80	—	—	—	—
'Coffee rust' Programme	3.40	1.0	30	2.00	04.12.79

Purchase of goods and services	11.20	1.0	30	2.00	05.12.79
Purchase of machinery spares and raw materials	8.40	1.0	20	2.00	11.11.80
Telecommunications	2.80	1.0	20	2.25	11.11.80
ITALY	55.00	—	—	—	—
Geothermal Project 'Momotombo I'	24.60	2.0	10	4.00	07.11.80
Geothermal Project 'Momotombo I'	5.40	2.0	12	4.00	07.11.80
Geothermal Project 'Momotombo II'	25.00	—	—	—	—
NETHERLANDS	83.30	—	—	—	—
Import of goods and services	17.50	8.0	23	2.50	22.10.80
Drinking water	5.00	4.0	23	2.50	21.02.81
Hospital and health centre	5.00	4.0	23	2.50	21.02.81
Grain storage system	1.90	8.0	30	2.50	03.11.81
Dredging port of Corinto	4.60	8.0	30	2.50	03.11.81
Agricultural inputs	2.00	8.0	30	2.50	03.11.81
Purchase of towing equipment	1.60	5/10	9-21	11-75-11	05.09.82
Port equipment and inputs	8.60	—	—	—	1983
Acquisition of goods and services	8.50	7.0	30	2.50	20.01.83
Finance for required goods and services	8.50	7.0	30	2.50	30.06.83
Acquisition of goods and services	1.30	—	8.5	10.37	24.01.84
Acquisition of goods and services	1.70	—	8.5	10.37	07.02.84
Improvement and enlargement of bridges	2.90	8.0	30	2.50	22.08.84
Agricultural development	1.00	8.0	30	2.50	22.08.84
Basic grains contingency plan	2.80	8.0	30	2.50	22.08.84
Agriculture and ports	6.80	8.0	30	2.50	04.06.85
'Daf' trucks	3.30	8.0	50	2.50	04.06.85
SPAIN	108.10	—	—	—	—
Machinery, equipment, raw materials, consumer goods	25.00	—	1-3-7	8.25	01.12.81
Machinery, equipment for Malacatoya and San Antonio sugar mills	13.10	—	5/8	10	1982
Import of spare parts, consumer goods, equipment	35.00	—	—	—	1983
Miscellaneous	35.00	—	—	—	11.85
SWEDEN	9.50	—	—	—	—
Purchase of sugar milling equipment	4.30	—	7	1.25	11.02.83
Extension of purchase of sugar milling equipment	0.50	—	7	1.25	01.03.84
Mining equipment and materials	4.40	—	2	14.00	12.02.85
Cattle raising equipment	0.30	—	2	14.00	12.02.85
CANADA	23.30	—	—	—	—
Agricultural projects	10.40	10	50	—	26.01.84
Promotion of water development	5.30	10	40	—	24.10.84
Geothermal Project 'Momotombo II'	7.60	10	50	—	05.10.85

Source: Ministry of External Cooperation.

APPENDIX IV: PRINCIPAL PROJECTS FINANCED BY WESTERN EUROPE AND CANADA

PRINCIPAL PROJECTS FINANCED BY WESTERN EUROPE AND CANADA

The following list is based on various inventories maintained in Nicaragua. The projects are registered in the Nicaraguan Annual Economic Plan, supported by Western Europe, Canada and certain multilateral sources. **Note:** the information is partial, reflecting the limited statistical information available. Nevertheless, the list gives an idea of the sectors targeted and the major sources of aid.

I. Projects Under Way in 1986

Project	Region*	Executor	Donor	Observations
Drinking water (17 communities)	National	INAA	Netherlands	Loan $538,000
Drinking water (Phase III)	I	INAA	COSUDE	Grant $469,000
Drinking water (Boaco)	V	INAA	UNO	Loan $2,496,000
Rural drinking water	Matagalpa	INNA	CARE	Grant $241,000
Drinking water	Managua	INAA	Canada	Credit $2,000,000
Drinking water	Z.E. III	INAA	UNICEF	Grant $469,000
Geothermal plant	II	INE	Canada	Loan $2,496,000
Electricity	III	INE	BCIE	Loan $1,530,000
Hydro-electric power (Asturias)	VI	INE	IDB	Loan $7,702,000
Mining (El Limón)	II	INMINE	Sweden	Grant $957,000
Mining (La Libertad)	V	INMINE	Sweden	Grant $638,000
Fishing, Co-op	II	INPESCA	Norwegian Popular Aid	Grant $1,064,000 Construction, buildings for receiving, freezing fish products
Fishing, 'Promar'	Z.E. II	INPESCA	IDB	Loan $4,865,000 Rehabilitation fishing fleet; acquisition new boats
Fishing, 'Copesnica'	Z.E.II	INPESCA	IDB	Loan $2,121,000 Acquisition new boats
Fishing, 'Alinsa'	II	INPESCA	IDB	Loan $419,000 Acquisition new boats; enlargement buildings
Fishing, 'Pescasa'	Z.E. II	INPESCA	IDB	Loan $1,858,000 Improvements, fishing fleet

Forestry seed bank	National	IRENA	DANIDA	Grant $50,000
Forestry bank	National	IRENA	SIDA	Grant $490,000 $155,000 being negotiated
Forestry bank	National	IRENA	IDB	Loan $2,449,000
Rehabilitation of slaughterhouses	National	MIDINRA	France	Credit $1,100,000
Replacement industrial machinery, equipment	National	MIDINRA	Denmark	Grant $1,300,000
Activities supporting agrarian reform	National	MIDINRA	EEC	Grant $500,000
Rehabilatation dairy plants	National	MIDINRA	Finland, WFP	Credit $954,000
Basic grains	National	MIDINRA	France	Credit $835,000
Dairy farm, 'Chiltepe'	III	MIDINRA	CIDA, Canada, IDB & others	Milk $25,000,000
'Valle de Sebaco'	VI	MIDINRA	Bulgaria, Spain	Agro-industry
Sugar complex, 'Victoria de Julio'	III	MIDINRA	Spain, Cuba, USSR, Mexico, France, Brazil, Sweden, Austria & E. Germany	$230,000,000
Integrated rural development (Stage II, Waslala)	VI	MIDINRA	EEC	$721,000 Integration of Waslala into national economy
Food programme (Jalapa)	I	MIDINRA	Netherlands	Loan $900,000 Food security
Integrated development (Valle de la Vigia)	I	MIDINRA	France	$450,000, $800,000 under negotiation Creation of cooperative development zone
Palm oil	Z.E. II & III	MIDINRA	Netherlands, France	7,000 ha. palm plantations
Irrigated basic grains production	National	MIDINRA	Spain, France & Brazil	Food security
Asphalt and emulsifier plant	IV	MICONS	Denmark	Loan $2,831,000
Road construction (Río Blanco-Siuna)	Z.E. I & IV	MICONS	IDB, Netherlands	Loan $11,600,000
Storage, procurement facilities (San Carlos)	IV	MICONS	Italy	Construction, storage centres
Texnisa	III	MIND	France, USSR	Textile enterprise

Transportation equipment	National	MIND	France	Credit $587,000
Oral rehydration salts	IV	MIND	France	Credit $131,000
Repair, acquisition of port equipment	IV	MITRANS	Netherlands	Grant $70,000, Loan $937,000
Navigation improvement	National	MITRANS	Netherlands	Grant $32,000, Loan $142,000
Dock repair (San Juan del Sur)	IV	MITRANS	Netherlands	Grant $24,000
Port construction (Puerto Lacustre)	Z.E. III	MITRANS	Netherlands	Loan $180,000
Pier reconstruction (Arlen Siu)	V	MITRANS	Netherlands	Grant $297,000, Loan $1,300,000
Pier reconstruction (Puerto Cabezas)	Z.E. I	MITRANS	Netherlands	Loan $692,000
Airport (Puerto Cabezas)	Z.E. I	MITRANS	Finland	Loan $475,000
Maintenance, repair digging equipment	Z.E. I	MITRANS	Netherlands	Grant $6,000, Loan $150,000
Pronorte	I	Sociedad Anónima Regional	BCIE, IFAD	Integrated rural development programme

* Regional boundaries correspond roughly with the departmental boundaries. Region I: Nueva Segovia, Madriz, Estelí; Region II: Chinandega, León; Region III: Managua; Region IV: Carazo, Granada, Rivas, Masaya; Region V: Chontales, Boaco; Region VI: Matagalpa, Jinotega; Zona Especial I and II: Zelaya; Zona Especial III: Río San Juan.

II. Large Investment Projects Completed by 1986

Project	Region*	Executor	Donor	Observations
Grain storage system (MASA)	II, III, IV & V	ENABAS, MICOIN	BCIE	C$316,000,000** $16,100,000
Geothermal plant Momotombo I	II	INE	GIE, BCIE, FIV, Italy & Canada	C$396,300,000, $85,300,000
Energy project (ninth)	National	INE	IBRD, BCIE	C$139,600,000, $24,600,000 Installation electricity, interconnection with Costa Rica, 5 new substations
Fishing, 'Copescosa'	IV	INPESCA	IBRD, FED, FIV & Peru	C$23,400,000, $4,210,000 Construction fishery
Pine forest (Nueva Segovia)	I	IRENA	Sweden	
Road construction (Tuma-Waslala-Siuna)	VI, Z.E. I	MICONS	OPEC	C$358,000,000, $37,600,000 208 km. road
Children's hospitals	III, IV & VI	MINSA	Netherlands	C$264,300,000, $4,400,000 Construction 4 hospitals
Railroad (Corinto-Chinandega)	II	MITRANS	Spain	C$158,600,000, $9,600,000 22 km. railroad
Chinorte (first stage)	II	SAR	Switzerland	Integrated development, road construction

* Regional boundaries correspond roughly with the departmental boundaries. Region I: Nueva Segovia, Madriz, Estelí; Region II: Chinandega, León; Region III: Managua; Region IV: Carazo, Granada, Rivas, Masaya; Region V: Chontales, Boaco; Region VI: Matagalpa, Jinotega; Zona Especial I and II: Zelaya; Zona Especial III: Río San Juan.

** C$ = Nicaraguan córdobas.

APPENDIX V: ANALYSIS OF AID CHANNELLED THROUGH THE AUGUSTO CÉSAR SANDINO FOUNDATION (FACS) 1982—MID-1986

ANALYSIS OF AID CHANNELLED THROUGH THE AUGUSTO CÉSAR SANDINO FOUNDATION (FACS) 1982—MID-1986

I. Origin of Aid via FACS by Country*

(U.S. dollars)

Country	Completed Projects (received)	Projects Under Way (requested)	Total
Australia	14,203	29,860	44,063
Belgium	159,081	1,114,428	1,273,509
Canada	2,752,242	426,173	3,178,415
Denmark**	59,443	25,317	84,760
France	44,676	484,847	529,523
Germany	762,904	2,186,111	2,949,015
Ireland	55,717	54,080	109,797
Italy	24,100	9,000	33,100
Mexico	16,693	—	16,693
Netherlands**	981,824	359,769	1,341,593
New Zealand	29,858	35,564	65,422
Norway	67,811	767,570	835,381
Spain**	19,202	6,867	26,069
Sweden	535,852	21,000	556,852
Switzerland	195,290	193,342	388,632
United Kingdom	244,306	155,363	379,669
United States	438,960	579,409	1,018,369
Total	**6,382,162**	**6,448,700**	**12,830,862**

Source: based on inventories provided by FACS.

* Excludes the value of much of the aid in kind.

** Excludes small amounts of institutional support.

II. Aid via FACS by Social Economic Sector*
(U.S. dollars)

Sector	Completed Projects (received)	Projects Under Way (requested)	Total
Health and sanitation	1,489,669	217,877	1,707,546
Education and training	1,102,158	605,099	1,707,257
Production	1,107,022	1,905,603	3,012,625
Emergency aid for war damage, refugees displaced by war	612,940	503,732	1,116,672
Supply and distribution networks	52,277	74,645	126,922
Food, nutrition, child welfare	1,223,878	1,791,385	3,015,263
Aid to disabled revolutionary fighters	44,879	27,200	72,079
Improvements in working and living conditions	48,405	1,030,794	1,079,199
Cultural and recreational facilities	521,640	164,827	686,467
Support for FACS	116,000	60,412	176,412
Research	63,294	67,126	130,420
Total	**6,382,162**	**6,448,700**	**12,830,862**

Source: based on inventories provided by FACS.

*Excludes the value of much aid in kind.

III. Nicaraguan Organizations Receiving Aid via FACS*

(U.S dollars)

Organization	Completed Projects (received)	Projects Under Way (requested)	Total
AMNLAE	828,678	171,252	999,930
ANDEN	74,327	—	74,327
ANS	36,392	37,418	73,810
ASTC	9,500	—	9,500
ATC	853,245	249,655	1,102,900
CDS	481,140	383,628	864,768
CST	175,569	35,375	210,944
FACS	165,157	139,958	305,115
FETSALUD	283,474	65,363	348,837
INNICA/popular organizations of the Atlantic Coast	78,136	83,316	161,452
INSSBI	1,556,943	1,733,490	3,290,433
JRM	20,868	—	20,868
Juventud Sandinista	134,645	8,400	143,045
Organization of Disabled Revolutionaries	44,879	13,200	58,079
SAMU	60,361	—	60,361
UNAG	683,458	3,006,315	3,689,773
Municipal authorities	86,045	—	86,045
Ministries	711,713	481,330	1,193,043
Regional governments	97,632	40,000	137,632
Total	**6,382,162**	**6,448,700**	**12,830,862**

Source: based on inventories provided by FACS.

* Excludes the value of much aid in kind.